THE DEVIL WITHIN

THE DEVIL WITHIN

Malcolm Alker
with Julie Stott

Scratching Shed Publishing Ltd

First published by Scratching Shed Publishing Ltd in 2012
Registered in England & Wales No. 6588772.
Registered office:
47 Street Lane, Leeds, West Yorkshire. LS8 1AP

www.scratchingshedpublishing.co.uk

ISBN 978-0956804334

Cover photography and design © Barney Allen

Unless stated otherwise, all other photographs © Malcolm Alker

A catalogue record for this book is available from the British Library.

Typeset in Cheltenham Bold and Palatino

Printed and bound in the United Kingdom by
L.P.P.S.Ltd, Wellingborough, Northants, NN8 3PJ

Dedications

MALCOLM

I dedicate this book to my gorgeous wife Sonia and brilliant kids, Mason and Madison. I would like to thank them for all the joy they have brought to my life - and also apologise for all the misery I've brought to theirs!

Seriously though, without Sonia I might be in jail by now. I was crazy at times as a youngster. Sonia reeled me in and stopped me going off the rails. I'll be eternally grateful for that, even though I do jokingly tell her it feels as if she's got a noose around my neck. Our family honestly wouldn't survive without Sonia; she holds us all together. I've been working seriously long hours over the past few months and can only do that because Sonia is looking after our children and doing a million other jobs around the house, as well as working full-time herself. I don't tell her often enough, but hopefully she now knows how much I love her.

As for Mason and Madison, it's impossible to say how much they mean to me. I just hope that when they grow up and read this they'll respect me for being so honest with this book of do's and don'ts - and remember not to follow my example with the don'ts. Love you, kids.

JULIE

For my fantastic sons, Calum and Robbie.

Contents

Acknowledgements

I am extremely grateful to my co-writer Julie Stott for her magnificent work in helping me to put this book together. I must also say a big thank you to Geoff Burrow and the players' union GMB, for all their financial and practical assistance.

Julie Stott fell in love with rugby league in 1984-85, when she covered Dewsbury home and away as Sports Editor of the *Dewsbury Reporter*. She has reported on the game on a daily basis since 2003, initially for *The Sun*, before taking over as rugby league correspondent of the *News of the World* in 2009. Currently, she is the *Daily Star*'s rugby league reporter.

*

Foreword
by Adrian Morley

When I think of Malc Alker, the word that immediately comes to mind is honesty. Honesty is a great trait to have in the game of rugby league, arguably the toughest team sport in the world. If you're not honest with your team-mates, or more importantly yourself, then you're in trouble.

For someone to be named Super League Hitman of the Year four times (an award given annually to the player who makes the most tackles in a season) is incredible. It is an achievement that tells you his commitment, toughness and honesty can never be questioned.

I learnt from my late team-mate, Terry Newton, that things weren't always so rosy for Malc and that in their junior team, Wigan St Judes, he would struggle to get in the side. So for someone who maybe wasn't as naturally talented or as big and strong as the other lads to go on and carve out the professional career he did, gives me even more respect for his determination.

Salford recognised Malc's leadership qualities at a very early age and made him club captain, a position he held virtually until he finished playing. He stayed with Salford through thick and thin, sometimes being the only shining light in a poor side. It was no secret that other clubs wanted to sign Malc, including teams from down under, which is a testament to his loyalty to the Reds.

Being a Salford lad I still live in the area and my little girl goes to the same nursery as Malc's daughter. Malc is a great bloke and I often see him doing the nursery run and occasionally in the local pub! Malc may not have been born in Salford, but he's Salford through and through and the people of the city have made him one of their own.

Adrian Morley, March 2012

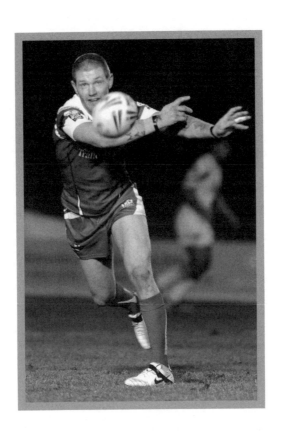

1

*

Tackling my Demons

My name is Malcolm Alker and when I was a Super League player I used to be addicted to drugs. In fact, BECAUSE I was a Super League player.

It may sound like I'm sitting in some sort of addicts' meeting, confessing all, and I guess I am really. But the thing that's even more shocking is the reality that there are, and have been, scores of Super League players just like me.

And none of us have run the risk of failing a drugs test, because it's all perfectly legal. The drugs that I and lots of other players got hooked on are prescription pain-killers. But let nobody be mistaken - if abused, they can end up taking over your life to the extent that you don't believe you can play without them. That's the sort of pressure that rugby league can apply. I know, because I got caught up in that nightmare. It's something that needs tackling before the problem gets out of hand. If it hasn't done so already.

If anybody doubts how serious this problem is, let me tell you of the horrors I suffered going through cold turkey when I came off the drugs once my career at Salford was finished.

Even now I can vividly remember the dreadful feeling of waking up at night sweating like a glass blower's backside, absolutely soaked from head to toe, with the depressing knowledge that I still wasn't over the worst.

I would look at the alarm clock and see it was only half an hour since last I'd looked; yet it felt as if I'd spent all night tossing and turning. And this was after yet another day of walking round like a bear with a sore head, snapping at anybody who said or did the slightest thing to irritate me. And it wasn't just that day. I'd gone through days and days of this torture, feeling that my body no longer belonged to me. 'I can't do this,' I'd mutter to myself for the umpteenth time, knowing full well that I simply had to if I was ever going to escape this hell. Cold turkey you see is like that - it's an agony that tests your willpower to its very limits.

As a player, I'd prided myself on having the ability to withstand the sort of pain and physical tiredness that would bring most people to their knees. But this was something else altogether.

Now, I know many people associate cold turkey with junkies. And yes, I'll hold my hands up and say I did feel like a junkie. Yet I wasn't some secret drug-taker, hooked on banned social or performance-enhancing drugs - what I had been doing was all perfectly above board. And, as I said, I certainly wasn't alone.

Look at any Super League team right now and there will be players who have fallen into the same mixed-up, crazy habits that I did. Just like me, these lads - and there are an awful lot of them - are playing with their health and possibly their sanity too, just so they can keep training and playing and keep hold of their shirt.

It's the price many players pay to have the sort of career

that most people can only dream of. And none of them are running the gauntlet of getting caught by the drug testers because prescription pain-killers are legal.

So if it's all okay, why am I here, shaking and sweating, well into my second week of cold turkey hell? The answer is because I, like lots of others, simply didn't know when to stop popping those magic pills. It starts off as one or two to dull aches and pains after a match. But gradually, as the pain is so much easier to handle after swallowing those little yellow and green tablets, it becomes one or two per day.

And hey, if a couple a day are helping, then maybe I need a couple more just to make sure that I play well? Why not? It's not illegal. is it? But hang on, the Tramadol tablets are making me a bit hyperactive and wired so I'm not going to be able to sleep. No worries, a couple of sleeping pills will sort that out.

So it goes on until you convince yourself that you will never be able to train or play, or even get out of bed, without them. It's like being in a washing machine cycle and you cannot see a way out of the problem. Stop the pills and you're convinced you'll be in too much agony to get in the team. And if you're not in the team, then your earnings are at risk. How could you look in your wife and kids' eyes, knowing that you'd let them down?

Of course, while all this is going on, a lot of players don't really see it as a problem if it's helping them to keep their shirt and therefore put food on the family table. And don't get me wrong, I know that I stole the last couple of years of my career thanks to Tramadol because, without those pain-killers, I would have really struggled to carry on.

I look back now and wonder how I let myself become addicted. And I thank God that I had the strength to get myself off them. My wife Sonia doesn't know this but she was the inspiration - or rather shock treatment - that I needed to clean up my act. When my career at Salford ended I went off the rails completely, and I do mean completely. I'd hardly been a clean-living sort of bloke, but not having a job to get up for every day totally and utterly floored me. The way Salford let me go was one of the most bitter and gut-wrenching things I'd ever suffered, but I'll go into that in more detail later.

Suffice to say, I started going out on benders that would last for days. I'd leave home on the Saturday, tell Sonia I'd see her later that night and wouldn't turn up again until the Tuesday. I wouldn't have much of a clue where I'd been or what I'd done, so you can imagine the ear-bashings I got when I eventually turned up home again.

I'm ashamed to say I've put Sonia through more than her fair share of worries over the years, but she's a fairly feisty character who can usually put me in my place. But this was different. Not only was I going missing on drink and drugs, I was depressed and wallowing in my own misery because I'd lost the career I'd had since being a teenager.

I felt Salford had thrown me out into the wilderness and I was embarrassed. But rather than face up to the problem, I'd seek salvation down the boozer. Every time Sonia told me I was out of order, we'd end up arguing and I'd storm off out on another bender and go missing for a few more days.

I knew Sonia was worried about me, about how we were going to look after our two kids and what the future held, but that didn't seem to matter when I viewed it through the bottom of a pint glass and with the help of my magic pills. Then, one day, I turned up home and Sonia just said: 'Don't leave us.' I looked at her and couldn't believe I'd gone so far off the rails that she thought I'd dump her and our kids.

It was only three words but they brought me to my senses with all the ferocity of a punch in the face. I couldn't believe I'd almost thrown away my marriage because I couldn't control my prescription drug taking or drinking - an awful cocktail. I didn't even need the drugs because I'd had a pain-killing injection in a long-standing neck injury so there wasn't even any pain there. That's how stupid it had become. I just thought I was reliant on them.

I didn't tell Sonia, but I vowed there and then that I had to face up to my problems and that was the day I stopped behaving like a maniac. She'll only realise when she reads this, but she brought me to my senses. I went out and had LOVE tattooed on my knuckles because Sonia had made me realise that love, not benders, was going to get me through this. If ever I started to doubt it, I'd only have to look at my hand for a swift reminder.

I collected all my Tramadol and sleeping pills, put them in a bag and threw them in a bin.

Which is how I ended up walking around the Trafford Centre one day looking like I'd just been for a swim fully-clothed. I was with my good pal and former Salford team-mate Paul Highton. He said: 'What's wrong, Malc?', as I ducked into a toilet for the umpteenth time.

'I'm going cold turkey and this time it's for good,' I said.

Paul instantly knew what I was going through because he'd had to do it himself at one point. You'd be amazed, you really would, at just how many players have either had to wean themselves off pain-killers or will be facing that agony at some time in the future. It's absolutely rife.

Anyway, before long, I'd sussed out where every single toilet was in the Trafford Centre. I was sweating so much my shirt was sopping and I had to take it off and try to dry it under the driers. I got a few funny looks, I can tell you.

And I'll not deny that it was bloody hard work. If I hadn't thrown the drugs away, I might have been tempted to pop a few, just to stop the shakes and sweating, not to mention the sudden rages I'd fly into. The number of drivers who got nasty hand signals from me over the two weeks it took me to recover is frightening.

But through it all I would look at Sonia and our kids and know it had to be done. If I'd really wanted to start again, it would have been easy, because there are plenty of players I could have phoned up and blagged a few tablets off. But I'd got to the point where I knew my life was nearly out of control. I'd almost lost my marriage. No way was I going to start again.

I'd never made a secret of being on prescription drugs, but didn't tell a lot of people I had come off them, yet it was staggering how many noticed. Members of my family began to comment on how I seemed more with it and not as gaunt or spaced-out as I used to be. The thing is, I never even realised I was spaced-out - you just don't notice the affect they are having on you.

This is a hell of a way to start a book that I also intend to be funny and entertaining. But I have done it deliberately because I really believe that the issue of prescription drugs is a ticking timebomb in our sport. I've thought long and hard about the problem and what should be done, and I'll go into all that in depth later.

Neither I nor, I'm sure, any other player who has faced this problem is looking for sympathy. We know that we live a lifestyle most blokes would give their right arm for. But I just wonder whether fans realise what Super League players put themselves through, and the risks some of them are taking with their health, in order to live that dream.

There is no doubt that pain-killers helped me to survive in one of the toughest team sports on the planet. But was it worth the price? I'm still trying to work that one out.

2

*

Booze, Baseball Bats
and a Broken Back

While prescription drugs helped me to prolong my career by a couple of years, there's no doubt what threatened to derail it - drink and my temper. Usually, the two went hand in hand.

Even I wince now at just how close I came to ending my playing days before they'd hardly started. I had signed for Salford at 16 and was made up because the coach was Andy Gregory; he had been one of my heroes. As a kid, I'd had many a happy time sitting on the wall at Central Park with my brother Melvin and my mates, watching Greg and the great Wigan teams.

Suddenly, here I was, training with fantastic players like Andy Platt, Steve Hampson, Paul Forber and Joe Faimalo. I loved it. I also began to go out drinking with them and being in that environment changed me into an adult very quickly. But soon my dream of becoming a household name just like those guys almost blew up in my face. And Salford probably still don't know how close I came to ruining everything.

The Devil Within

I was 17 and had gone to a pub near my home in Billinge for a pint or two with a mate. There were a few blokes there that I knew vaguely and everything was fine until one of them accused me of eyeing up his girlfriend. I swear I hadn't but as usual my fists were faster than my gob and a fight broke out. I'd always been brought up with a hit first, think later approach to trouble, so I was happy to get it on with this bloke because he was bang out of order.

Several more people joined in and the fight started getting pretty intense with bottles and glasses thrown and broken, before the pub staff managed to throw the other bloke and his mates out. There were loads of them, so the staff kept me inside to keep us apart. The uneasy calm didn't last long, though, because our next door neighbour was in the pub at the time and she phoned my dad saying: 'Your Malcolm's been in a fight and there might be more trouble.'

Given that it was my dad who had drummed the hit first motto into me from an early age, it was no surprise when he turned up minutes later waving a baseball bat. My brother Melvin was also tooled up with one and it was decided that me and this other bloke should sort it out once and for all, man-to-man, outside the pub.

I beat him pretty convincingly and me, Melvin and Dad drove home thinking it had all been settled. How wrong we were. About an hour later, we were aware of a commotion outside and looked out to see the same blokes, and a few others, yelling for me to come out. That was like a red rag to a bull to Dad. He opened the door and headbutted the nearest bloke he saw. It would have been a classic start to a fight if only he hadn't mis-timed his headbutt and broken his own nose instead of the other bloke's.

All hell broke loose as me, Melvin and my mum raced out to help Dad take on these fifteen blokes. The funniest thing, thinking about it now, is the sight of Mum fighting grown men in our front garden. She had just been about to go to bed and was in her dressing gown. But we don't call Mum the Tasmanian Devil for nothing! She's got a right temper on her (maybe that's where I get mine from) and none of us had a second thought about how she would cope. Dressing gown or not, we knew she could handle herself in a fight.

So, four of us against fifteen of them, but we did okay even though they were all adults and our Melvin was only 15 years old at the time. Mum's dressing gown ended up covered in blood, the windows in the porch all got smashed and our white car, parked in the drive, was a red car by the end. The fight went on for quite a while until the police eventually came, sparking a mass disappearing act by our opponents.

What I hadn't realised was that I'd actually broken my back in two places and squashed two discs during the fight. By the time the police started to question us I could hardly stand up. We insisted that we didn't know who the other blokes were and thought that was the end of the matter - apart from my serious back injury, Dad's broken nose, several bumps and bruises and the damage to the house.

But it seemed that this lot were the sort to bear a grudge. Over the next three nights, ten to fifteen of them walked up and down past our house, trying to intimidate us. I couldn't move much by this stage and Dad didn't want to confront them again with the odds stacked so heavily against us. But he's not one to let things go, my dad, and on the fourth night he arranged for my uncles, their sons and mates to come to the house, so he could sort them out good and proper.

Our house looked like more like a scene in a riot movie, with nine of them waiting in the dark with hammers, pick-axes and whatever other weapons they could lay their hands on. They waited and waited but, for some unknown reason, the blokes didn't turn up that night - and they don't know how lucky there were! The battering they'd have got doesn't bear thinking about. There was talk about going out and trying to find them but, in the end, Dad and the rest of the family decided to let things be.

That was fine but, in the meantime, I had the massive problem of sorting my back out and trying to stop Salford from finding out about what had happened. It was that badly fractured I couldn't manage anything apart from daily trips to hospital for six months. I told the club that my back had been sore after the last game I'd played and that it had just got worse and they believed me. The club physio at the time, Linda McCarthy, also worked at Wigan Hospital and she was great because she oversaw my recovery. I'd go in most days and she'd get me in a giant sling so I could walk in a water pool. I looked like a bloody horse, prancing about, but it certainly helped get my back in shape.

Because we hadn't told the police who else had been involved - and to be truthful I didn't even know which bloke had done my back in - I was able to make a claim to the Criminal Injuries Board and ended up getting £3,500. It was good money at the time, but I realised I'd been really lucky that the injury wasn't even more serious for my career. I'd got away with a six-month lay-off and escaped a bollocking from the club because they didn't know the real reason.

Any sensible person would have taken that on board and calmed down a bit. But since when was I sensible? Mind you, one of the funniest reprimands I ever got over my drinking habits came from Andy Gregory.

Despite the scare of the back incident, I still continued to think I was fireproof when it came to heavy drinking. I've never really suffered with hangovers and have always been able to train hard the next day, no matter how much of a skinful I've had the night before. I used to think it was fantastic that I could do both to the maximum, but maybe I'd have been better off if I had suffered a few more rough mornings. Anyway, one day I got a message that Greg wanted to see me and wanted my dad to come as well. The warning bells went off a bit because I knew I was playing well - so well, in fact, that not long afterwards I was handed the captaincy at 19 years of age, so I knew he couldn't be hauling me over the coals for anything on the playing front.

Somebody must have told Greg that I was drinking a lot but, given the circumstances, it seemed a bit strange that he decided to have the meeting in the pub he owned at the time. Anyway, we got there and Greg and Dad immediately got themselves a pint of Guinness. Greg asked if I wanted one as well. Never one to turn a pint down, I said yes. We sat down and Greg started to tell me I was drinking too much. It's a bit hard to accept a bollocking about your drinking habits when you and the coach are discussing it over a pint, but I wasn't going to quibble.

And then, with the bollocking out of the way, we carried on chatting, and drinking, and drinking until it turned into a right old session. So much so that I ended up being sick in the toilets of Greg's own pub. His lecture about drinking hadn't really had the right effect. I will always be grateful to Greg for signing me and he did a lot for me as a person and a player. But even I have to admit that he wasn't always the best role model.

That first session wasn't the first we had together. One night I was so drunk I ended up having to crash at his house. The next morning we had training but I didn't have my kit, so I had to borrow some off Greg. That was one day I did actually feel ill, but I could hardly get told off when I started spewing up on the training field. I'd been on a night out with the coach and was wearing his kit; the best excuse a player's ever had.

Big brother - we have always been a tight-knit family

3

*

Hit First, Think Later

Recently, I went on a caravan holiday to Cornwall with Sonia, my seven-year-old son Mason and two-year-old daughter Madison. Mum and Dad joined us for the last few days as they often do. I was watching Dad play with Mason and heard him say something that instantly took me right back to when I was Mason's age.

'Hit first, think later,' my dad told him. And with those four little words I was a kid again, experiencing my first harsh lesson in how to fight and how not to fight.

We lived in Higher Ince, Wigan, at the time. I had been playing in the back alleys and got into a scuffle with this lad, who belted me one. I went home blubbing, hoping no doubt to get a cuddle and a bit of sympathy. But instead I walked straight into another belting from Dad.

He grabbed a pillow and started hitting me with it, shouting: 'Get back out there and batter that lad! Don't come home until you do.' I was hysterical. Although I was scared of the kid who'd hit me, I was more frightened that Dad really wouldn't let me come home again. I left the house with tears pouring down my face. I was crying so much my chest was heaving with sobs by the time I eventually saw the other lad. I can vividly remember the look of amusement on his face when he saw me walking up to him in a right state - and the look of shock when I went straight up and hit him. I was still crying but I was so scared of Dad that I gave the kid a pasting.

I went home and told Dad, who said: 'Well done son. I'm proud of you.' It felt so good and from there, the fighting has never really stopped. Dad always taught me, rightly or wrongly, that you've got to get in first and worry about the consequences afterwards because, if not, you might end up on the wrong end of a good hiding. And that principle has not done me too badly - sort of!

Neither Mum or Dad are ones to give out advice and not follow it themselves. They can both handle themselves and many a time I remember them going out to a boozer to watch a cabaret, as they did in those days, and Dad would come home with his shirt ripped and his knuckles bruised. The Tasmanian Devil usually wasn't very far behind.

And then there's our Melvin to throw into the mix. Growing up with a kid brother like him was always going to make life one hell of a scrap. Melvin is 18 months younger than me and was a right little shit from the start. Since that first fight, I've always loved scrapping but Melvin was on a different scale. He's a total head-the-ball and the number of fights I've had to join in that Melvin started is unbelievable. Right from being little he'd get into fights just for the hell of it. One year, I remember him standing on the dance floor of this holiday camp we were staying at, ripping off his shirt and challenging anyone and everyone to a fight.

He used to get into so much trouble and get so many good hidings off Dad that sometimes I would take the blame, even if it was Melvin's fault, just to give him a break from getting another hiding. Not that he was ever grateful, of course. One of his favourite tricks when we were kids was to start screaming and howling for no reason. When Dad came to see what the noise was, he'd say I'd thumped him and Dad would slap me across the back of the head.

Melvin just loves conflict and would never back down, even when he was clearly in the wrong. Many a time he'd get smacked and be crying his eyes out but would still be arguing. As he got older, he stopped the crying but still wouldn't back down. When he was about 13, he fed a tin of stewing steak to our pet doberman. Mum went absolutely berserk. Melvin looked her in the eye and denied he had done it, but Mum wasn't having any. She punched him so hard that she left an imprint of her ring on his cheek. It must have hurt like hell, but he didn't cry and still insisted he hadn't fed the dog.

As you can see, Mum and Dad had their hands full with us and they could both dish out the slipperings. But while it was accepted that we could fight and that we would get a battering if we overstepped the mark, Mum and Dad were extremely strict on other things. Our end terrace house was a decent one because Dad is a builder and joiner. He did a lot of work with my grandad and uncles, extending and doing it up. But there's no getting away from the fact that Higher Ince was a pretty rough area.

Nevertheless, Mum and Dad instilled good manners and right and wrong into us from being tots. I honestly didn't even think about stealing or causing damage, as a lot of kids do just for the hell of it. That sort of thing never entered our heads because of the way we were brought up. Fighting was acceptable but anything worse was frowned upon. Even so, there were plenty of calls from school complaining about my behaviour.

27

The Devil Within

When I was eight, I got into a scrap with a kid on the way home from school and pushed him over a wall. How was I to know there was a dog on the other side that would attack him? He only got bitten a couple of times, so it seemed a bit off that his parents should complain to the headmaster. As you can guess, the headmaster and my parents didn't share my views and I ended up getting a right flogging off Dad.

Another time the primary school head called Mum and Dad in was when the teachers caught me on the school roof. I couldn't see what they were worried about myself. How else was I going to get the football back? It wasn't as if any of the other kids were brave enough to climb up.

But on a few other occasions I did get away with stuff because Mum and Dad knew I hated bullies and was always happy to take them on and help their victims. Even school backed down on expelling me when I explained what had really happened in one particular lesson. We were doing RE at St Peters High School, Wigan, when a lad started picking on a kid with a hair lip. I told him to stop but he wouldn't so, in the middle of the lesson, I got up and punched him so hard it looked as if his eye was going to fall out. He was in a right mess and, at one point, they thought he was going to go blind in it. But after I explained the circumstances, the school gave me one month's isolation instead.

It was boring, sitting in the medical room on your own, having work brought to you, but I got used to it because I was in there that often. Another time, I got sent to the store-room to serve out my isolation and thought I'd come across a brilliant way to pass one of my exams. I was useless at French, but as I rummaged among the shelves (as you do) I came across the mock GCSE paper. My bubble of excitement didn't take long to burst though. None of the questions were in English and I couldn't understand enough to cheat.

It was between me and another lad as to who was the

cock of the school. It annoyed me that people might think it was him. But anyone who did quickly changed their mind after one IT lesson. I wasn't good at IT and couldn't work out who had sent an abusive message to my screen. I asked the lad sitting next to me, who worked out it was my rival in the hardness stakes. So I immediately jumped up and pasted him as he sat at his desk. I know I should have waited until after school but I never think that way. I have to act straight away if I'm standing up for myself or somebody else.

I still don't know how I managed it, but I kept myself out of trouble in my last school year and actually came out with some decent results - one 'B', six 'C's, a 'D' and an 'E' (in French). The teachers were as surprised as me; I'm sure most of them still remember me for my fiery temper. As I said, it could go off with the slightest provocation and still does. There have been a few times when, later, I've realised that I could have easily ended up in trouble with the police. But when the red mist comes down it does so with a vengeance.

Like the time some teenagers tried to force their way into our house when Sonia opened the door to them. It appeared they had lost a Staffordshire bull terrier called Taz and had been wandering around when they saw our pet Staffie in our garden - bizarrely also called Taz. They assumed we had nicked their dog, knocked on the door and, when Sonia opened it, tried to force their way in, shouting and bawling. Sonia somehow managed to push them out again but she was really shaken by the shock of the incident and was in a right state when she phoned to tell me what had happened. I was on a club promotion with the then-coach John Harvey but dropped everything and raced home. Steam was coming out of my ears at the thought of somebody scaring Sonia, trying to take my dog and invading our privacy. When I reached home, I immediately grabbed a baseball bat and went hunting everywhere. Somebody told me where they lived, so I gave them a dose of their own medicine and barged straight in through the front door. I know that was stupid, I was doing exactly what they had annoyed me by doing, but I wanted them to feel as afraid as Sonia had been. The kids' parents were in at the time and you can imagine how angry they were, but eventually it all calmed down and they got their lads to apologise. I know I could have ended up in trouble, but not half as much bother as those boys would have been in if I'd been in my house when they tried to get in. No one threatens my family and gets away with it.

On a less serious note, I've also handed out some rough justice to kids who have dared to mess with my property. Shortly after me and Sonia got our first home in Tyldesley, it was New Year's Eve. We don't really like celebrating the New Year so had gone to bed early. I was laying there in my boxer shorts when I heard a commotion outside. I looked out to see three drunken kids, aged about 16 or 17, tipping over our bin and kicking everything around.

I was livid but rather than knock on the window decided to race out of the house in only my boxers and with nothing on my feet to confront them. They legged it down the road but, fuelled by anger, I was faster and grabbed hold of the first one I could catch, yelling at the other two to come with me as well. They were so shocked they gave up easily and meekly came back, where I stood over them as they picked everything up and put it back in the bin. At the time, I was really into weightlifting and eating a dozen eggs a day, so you can imagine how many broken shells there were. I was dying to laugh as the lads grovelled around, but instead managed to stay looking mean.

Another time some kids were left with egg on their faces - literally - was when they threw one at my window while I sat watching telly. Once again I was only in my boxers. I was on good money then, so we could have the heating on all the time. Now I'm a normal working bloke, I tell Sonia to put her coat on if she's cold. And there's no sitting about in boxers anymore either. Anyway, once again my temper went from zero to 100 in a nano-second and I was out of the house chasing the lads for all I was worth. When they raced down an alley I had to let them go; the ground was just too rough and dangerous for me to run in barefeet. Most people would have given up at this point, but I can't let things lie like that. I went back home, got some clothes on and went out in the car, driving around for ages. Eventually I saw the culprits in a shop and went in and asked if they'd been throwing eggs.

'Course not,' came the quick answer. 'It wasn't us.'

But then I noticed one of the lads was holding something under his top and pushed him hard in the chest. My hunch was right. To my delight he was hiding a load of eggs which were now smashed up and dripping down his body.

How I react sometimes is maybe wrong, but I have never and still don't start fights. I'm just very happy to end them.

Dark secret - rugby league can be a lonely place

4

*

Human Growth Hormone

A ctually, when I said earlier that I've always known right from wrong and have usually stuck by those rules, I am now going to make a confession.

It's a pretty big and pretty shameful one. And it's a secret that not even my family are aware of until now. I know this will shock and disappoint them, but if I'm writing my book there is no point in not being totally honest.

I'm putting my reputation on the line by saying this, but a number of years ago I took a couple of courses of human growth hormone. Yes, I knew full well that was cheating but, at the time, I couldn't be arsed. I wanted an advantage, pure and simple. And, if it had worked better for me than it did, I would have taken it for a lot longer. Like any other player on it, I was confident I wouldn't get caught.

Sadly, in rugby league, the words human growth hormone now go hand-in-hand with the tragedy of Terry Newton, who was banned for taking it and, seven months later in 2010, committed suicide. It's no wonder, then, that many people see it as a curse and something to be stamped out of our game. Rightly so. But back in 2003, when I took it, players thought it was completely undetectable and a fairly easy way to make you stronger and help you play better.

By then, I'd been hearing people talk about it for a couple of years or so and knew some were taking it because of the benefits. If you are aware of what to look for, the symptoms of someone taking HGH are fairly easy to spot. Their body becomes more defined. The chin becomes wider. You can develop a growth on the back of your heel and the forehead immediately above the eyebrows is more pronounced. Apart from the physical changes, HGH takers start training and playing a lot better than they have been doing previously.

I watched, listened and knew that players had been dope-tested while on HGH, and nothing had shown up, so I decided to give it a try. But while I wasn't bothered that it was classed as cheating, I wasn't so callous that it didn't worry me a bit. I certainly wasn't going to tell Sonia. Even if I didn't think it was wrong, Sonia certainly would and she would have left me in no doubt that I was being stupid.

So there I was, with my conscience on a guilt trip, but not bad enough to stop me ringing up a player I knew who was on it and who I was fairly certain would supply me. Even if he wouldn't, there were others. A fair few, in fact. When they read this, the Rugby Football League will no doubt want me to name names, but I would never do that. Just as it was my decision to take HGH, so it was other players' decision to do so. It's not up to anybody else to reveal their secrets. Nor is there anybody out there forcing players to gamble with their reputations and careers. We all did it completely voluntarily.

As it happened, when I phoned the player and told him I wanted a course he didn't bat an eyelid. He said it would cost £180 for a three-week course and told me when to pick it up and how to take it. It was like we were arranging to buy a TV or something. I didn't ask where he got it from because I didn't want to know. But that's another risk players take when they do this - who knows how pure or good it is? It's not as if you can ask for proof or demand your money back if you're not happy or suffer any side-effects.

I chose to start the course at the end of the 2003 season - we had six weeks off - and went to collect my first lot when Sonia was at work. I had a small fridge in the spare bedroom that I kept my protein drinks in and knew Sonia hardly ever looked in there. Mind you, it showed how jumpy I was that I hid them in a butty box behind the drinks.

The guy I got it off told me to inject the liquid into the body fat near my belly button every morning and night, Monday to Friday, for three weeks. But because I felt I had to sneak around so that my wife wouldn't catch me in the act, I decided it was safer to double up the dose and inject myself just once, in the middle of the day, when Sonia wasn't about. That's probably why it didn't work. I followed the routine but felt no benefit whatsoever. Worse, I lost weight instead of putting it on, unlike everyone else I knew who was taking it. Throughout my career, I've always had to be careful to stay at a decent weight. I couldn't believe it. There I was trying something I knew was wrong, that people would say was cheating, and the pounds were falling off.

I'd been training really hard on my own, probably harder than normal because I thought the HGH would be helping, so that maybe had something to do with the weight loss too. I phoned my supplier pal up again and arranged to pay for another three-week course, convinced that this time I'd start to see the benefits. Every day, I followed the injection routine but every time I weighed myself it was the same story. It was a nightmare. I'd lost about a stone at a time of year when I needed to be putting weight on. The new season was just around the corner. And that, I admit, is the only reason I

35

packed in the HGH. If I was a better person - or one who wanted to paint themselves in a better light - I'd probably say I'd come to my senses and realised that what I was doing was morally wrong and indefensible. But I'm nothing if not honest and, as I say, there's little point in writing an autobiography if you're not going to be truthful. Yes, I felt guilty. But I know I'd have carried on if it had worked.

However, if I had known then what would later happen to Terry I would never have taken it in a million years. And if HGH had been detectable in blood tests back then, there's no way I'd have run the risk. As it was, once I came off it I immediately put weight back on, but bad weight around my belly. I was worse off than before. That isn't an appeal for sympathy. I one hundred per cent don't deserve any.

As the years went on, more and more players began to use it because everyone was convinced it was foolproof. No one had been caught and you'd be surprised by some of the big names who were on it.

Personally, I was never tempted to try HGH again, but I always kept track of what was happening and followed developments into the testing of it on the internet. I was intrigued more than anything and eventually read that they had a discovered a test which, they claimed, could detect it in blood samples. Even so, the shock when Terry became the first professional sportsman in the world to be caught was unbelievable. He was a good mate and I would never blame him for taking it. That would be the pot calling the kettle black.

Rugby league puts enormous pressure on players to be the best and everyone wants to gain any advantage they can. Terry's death was enormously tragic and it's awful that it took something so bad to make people come to their senses. But Terry getting caught instantly stopped a lot of players from taking HGH. Suddenly everyone was afraid that they might be next and it cleaned the game up enormously.

But let's not be fooled. HGH may have joined anabolic steroids on the list of drugs most professional sportsmen would not dare take, but I'm sure something else will be developed in future. That's how things are in sport. The desire to succeed can over-rule honesty and integrity.

Melvin and me had a tough but loving upbringing

5

*

Happy Days

The murky and secretive world of illegal drugs was a world away from how I viewed rugby league as a kid. Born in 1978, I watched my Wigan heroes in awe as a youngster and could only dream of playing professionally.

It was a dream achieved by the skin of my teeth because, at first, I was all set to join the Navy. After leaving school, I researched it all, met the Naval advisers and decided that the open waters were for me. If Salford had come in for me two weeks later than they did I would have already signed up and been committed for the next several years.

Nobody in our family had been in the Navy before, so it's not as if I grew up listening to tales of the sea. The only reason I can think of for being so attracted to the water was the year we spent living on it. Mum and Dad were getting increasingly concerned that Higher Ince wasn't the sort of place they wanted to bring up their boys in. Michael, who is nine years younger than me, had just been born, so there were now three of us to keep an eye on.

The Devil Within

Two years later, Marlon came along too and by now you are probably wondering what this obsession is with names beginning with the letter 'M'. Well, I honestly have no idea. Dad's called Malcolm too, but it was our mum Jacqueline's idea to give us all 'M' names. Mum's always been a little strange. The again, maybe I am too, because I've done the same with Mason and Madison.

Anyway they wanted us to grow up in a better area but couldn't find a place that was right, so Dad decided to buy a boat instead. As you do. He bought an old trawler moored down at Salford Quays. But before you start thinking that we were a trendy family in the making, you'd better think again. This was long before the city planners cast their eye over the Quays and decided to turn it into a place for the designer pads of the rich and famous.

Back then, the whole area was completely derelict. The only neighbours we had were the rats that ran rife. It may sound horrendous, but when you are nine years old and daring, it was a world full of forbidden adventures and games. Next time you're down the Quays, have a look at the big old blue cranes that are still there; massive things that are used to haul boats out of the water. For me and Melvin they were the best climbing frames any kid could dream of.

Mum and Dad had no idea we climbed up them and, if they had, they would probably have had heart attacks. We are talking huge cranes here, but my brother and me would shin up to the top and gaze over Manchester, pretending we were kings of the whole city. Looking back, it's unbelievable what risks we were running, but it seemed like a bit of fun.

That whole experience was great for all of us, even though Mum had her hands full with the new baby and also had to take me and Melvin to our school, High Ince Primary, every day. Dad has always worked long days and he would then come home and do further work on the boat. It was a pretty big one, so there was lots to do, but we thought it was fantastic. There were four bedrooms, a kitchen, dining room, living room and wheelhouse.

The weird lifestyle brought us all really close together as we were so isolated. We didn't have any neighbours, apart from the rats, and Mum and Dad would spend loads of time playing with us. When the weather was good, we'd all take turns to jump off the top of the boat into the water and go swimming. Goodness knows what was in the water at that time; there's no way it would have been as clean as it is now. But we never bothered. We were living like gypsies and it felt like one long holiday for me and Melvin.

We were never bored. As well as the dodgy adventures we got up to around the Quays, Mum and Dad always made sure we had top things to play with. They can both be tough when it comes to dishing out the discipline, but they are also big softies at heart when it comes to kids. We were spoilt rotten, to be honest, and always seemed to have expensive remote-control cars, motorbikes, computers, you name it, before anyone else. They do the same thing now with all their grandkids; it's what they love doing. Dad pretends to go mad with Mum for spending so much money at birthdays and Christmas, but we all know that he's secretly chuffed they can spoil them.

After about a year afloat, Mum and Dad found a big three-bedroomed home in Billinge and they still live there now. It was weird getting used to living in a house again after the freedom we'd enjoyed at the boat, but the wooden floor boards in mine and Melvin's bedroom soon gave us a new game that would entertain us for hours. We'd both go barefoot and take it in turns to run across the room while one threw darts at the other one's feet. I don't think Mum and Dad were too thrilled by all the dart holes, but it was certainly better than getting one stuck in your foot.

The Devil Within

When we were little, we were both into wrestling and as a six-year-old I came second in the British Championships, so I was quite handy. To my mind, it was brilliant because it was fighting that you didn't get told off for. Mind you, it also gave me my first experience of how referees can ruin everything with one dodgy decision. I'd gone to Belgium with Mum for a competition over there and I was definitely winning my fight. I'd held my opponent down long enough but didn't get the decision. While I was wondering what had happened, the other lad turned me quickly and the ref gave the decision to him way before he should have. I was gutted and it turned me off the sport a bit because I couldn't believe that I could be cheated out of a win that was properly mine. Even now, I still can't be doing with injustices.

As we got older, my brother and me preferred boxing, but nothing official, just the stuff that used to wind Mum up when we kept wrecking the living room. We'd get mates round and box with our hands in pillows. We bought some boxing gloves after a while, but the dog chewed them up so it was back to the pillows. That meant, of course, that you didn't have the same protection - sometimes deliberately. I can remember one day making sure that there was hardly any material covering my knuckles and knocking one mate clean out with one punch. He broke the living room lamp as he collapsed. Mum wasn't too happy about that either.

Even though I fought a lot I was a pretty good kid really and quite mature for my age. Even at nine I can remember making Mum and Dad's breakfast for them on Sundays, or helping Mum around the house. But there was no doubt that I was lively and needed something positive in which to channel my energy. That's where rugby league came in.

Dad had played for the Wigan St Patricks amateur side, but never pushed any of us into playing and that's probably why I didn't get involved until the under-13s. I've taken the same approach with my lad, Mason. He's into football more than rugby because all his mates at school play it. He loves it and that's fine with me.

But probably because Dad didn't push us, I absolutely fell in love with rugby league as soon as I started training with Hindley Giants. Melvin came along too and one of the funniest things was seeing him put the ball into the scrum and then diving straight in to grab it again. Melvin is a lad who likes to play to his own rules.

Hindley was too far away to get to training easily so, after a while, we joined Orrell St James. But I'm certainly not going to kid you into thinking I was a budding star straight away. When you're winning games by 80-odd points every week you don't learn much, especially when you're stuck out on the wing like I was, just standing there watching other people do all the tackling and scoring all the tries.

Terry Newton was our hooker and you could tell, even at that age, that he was destined to make it. Warren Stevens, later of Warrington, was also in the side and along with those two there were quite a few dominant players meaning I never saw much of the ball. I was hacked off but knew I wanted to play, so I moved clubs again, this time joining Wigan St Pats' under-14s. We got stuffed most weeks but I loved it because I was involved and therefore learning tons.

I started out at loose forward for St Pats and then moved to hooker, where I knew I'd found my position. I'd regularly pester Dad to help me practise my tackling technique on the front lawn and quite often ended up hurt, but I couldn't get enough of it. Tackling was just instinctively my thing.

But even then, I was never the sort of player who people earmarked for success. It didn't bother me. I was enjoying myself too much and couldn't even bear to miss training. If Mum or Dad couldn't take me I'd cycle six miles there and home again. Getting home was a killer; uphill all the way.

The Devil Within

But nothing would stop me. We once went on holiday to Bulgaria and I got salmonella poisoning, but I insisted on going training when I got home, even though Mum and Dad told me not to. I got to training and played like a wet lettuce I was that ill, but I refused to give in until the coach ordered me to stop for my own good.

It was sheer guts and determination more than any great skill that won me a few club prizes at the end-of-season presentation nights. And I never got selected for any town or representative teams. As a result, I was convinced that I was just destined to be a decent club player, fitting in games around my time in the Navy.

But then luck - and Andy Gregory - came into my life.

6

*

Welcome to Salford
...with a Bollocking

I had never scored a try for Wigan St Pats and, as I said, I was never one of those players like Terry Newton who oozed class from an early age. But somebody must have been looking down on me the day Andy Gregory came to watch us play.

I honestly had no idea he was even there but, luckily for me, I had a blinder and scored two tries. I was pretty chuffed with myself anyway, but when Greg approached me afterwards it was like all my Christmases had come at once. I couldn't really believe that this man, the player who'd been my boyhood hero, was actually standing there and asking if I fancied signing for Salford! Oh, let me think for a.... well, yes, that does sound pretty good! As if there was ever any doubt.

Mum and Dad were away on holiday, so I told Greg I'd love to sign but would have to speak to them first. Waiting for them to come home was agony. What if Salford changed their minds? I was weeks away from joining the Navy but, suddenly, all that was forgotten. My brother, Melvin, went on to serve in the Navy for six years and Michael went in the Army for four. Hearing their tales, I know I would have loved that lifestyle. But choosing between the Navy and a rugby league career was a no-brainer.

By the time Mum and Dad got back I had discovered that Wigan and another club - I never found out who - were also interested, but Dad urged me to sign for Salford and put myself in the shop window, saying that if I was good enough I would prove myself to everybody. At a similar age, Dad could also have signed for either Salford or Huddersfield, but he turned them both down because he was earning good money in the building trade. I don't think he's ever regretted the decision because he's always done well for himself, but I know he was thrilled that I'd got my chance.

We told Salford that I was happy to join and on my 16th birthday me and my dad went down to the Willows for the official signing. It was pretty nerve-wracking. I was still having to pinch myself that the great Andy Gregory wanted me to play for his team. I signed for two-and-a-half years and got £2,500 up front, as well as a deal for match fees. At 16 years of age, you can imagine how good that felt.

I had to grow up fast in an environment that included great players like Steve Hampson and Andy Platt - and I do mean fast. I even got a bollocking in my first training session. We'd done the official ceremony on the pitch but it took longer than expected. Consequently, I was late getting to training with my new team-mates.

Nervously I jogged over, hoping to slip in quietly among them. Fat chance. As I ran up, they all started giving me abuse for my time-keeping. Later, I came to realise that was just the sort of banter you get all the time among groups of players. But, as a raw novice, I didn't know how to take it. For once in my life, I didn't have a gobby response. Dad was on the sidelines laughing at all the abuse I was copping, but I just stood there like a nervous, wet-behind-the-ears kid.

The players also didn't hang about in 'welcoming' me to the squad. I can remember a few times playing touch rugby when suddenly, from nowhere, a player would flatten you with a bone-crushing tackle that you didn't see coming. It was harsh, but it was the senior players' way of keeping you in your place and seeing how you handled it. When you eventually started fighting back, they knew they had done their job. It was like an apprenticeship and it doesn't happen these days, which is a pity.

Despite his long hours, Dad would always try his best to take me to training. But after a while we both knew it was too difficult for him to keep taking time off to ferry me about, so I joined Salford's apprentice scheme on £45 a week. One of the first jobs I was told to do was clean the first team players' boots and I refused. 'No way am I going to clean anybody else's boots,' I said, and there was no way they could get me to change my mind. 'Look,' I said. 'I'll sweep up or do anything else, but I'm not cleaning boots.' Once I've made my mind up, nothing will change it. Mind you, I didn't tell them the real reason: I wasn't going to clean another player's boots and make him look good, when I wanted to take his place in the team.

There were other things about the role that didn't bother me, even though kids who come through nowadays would be up in arms about them. One of the peculiarities of being an apprentice or academy player was the rule that you couldn't go into the first team changing room, even if you were training with them. I started training with the first team straight away but, for more than a year, I had to get changed in another room. And quite often that meant on my own, because I was regularly the only youngster who was allowed to train with them.

47

The Devil Within

I could hear all the banter in the next room as I got changed in silence, but I never got a cob on about it because I knew that you had to earn the right to be in there. It was a stern lesson but it made me more determined. That was the thinking in that era and I was fine with it. If I'd resented it and started feeling sorry for myself, I wouldn't have been the right sort of person who'd fight for his place in the team.

It's a different story nowadays. Young players get everything far too easily. And some of them complain like hell if they think they're not being treated on a par with the established players. When I started, it was my job to carry a massive water container out to the training pitches. It was an eight-minute walk from the changing rooms and by the end my arms were almost dropping off, the containers weighed so much. But I knew that it was my job, no arguing.

Towards the end of my career at Salford, we'd get kids like Richie Myler throwing their dummies out of the cot if they thought they were having to do something the senior players weren't. I'm glad to see Richie has matured since he went to Warrington and I'm sure that is partly to do with the shock of being dropped for the Challenge Cup final and then their last play-off match in 2010. The influence of a top bloke like Adrian Morley will also have done him a world of good.

I used to hate the attitude you'd get from some young players and, even at the end of my career, I'd tell the coach, on the quiet, to pick me out to do a menial job at training. I wanted to show the younger lads that everybody had to play their part, no matter who they were.

As a young player I knew I had to fight for everything. I loved training and always have done, but after a few months of travelling to Salford from Wigan and back, I was finding it increasingly difficult. It was costing me a bomb for one thing, so I quit the apprenticeship scheme and got a job in a Salford hat factory, along with academy player Lee Hudson.

I could have worked full-time for Dad but, from experience, knew what a slave-driver he can be. Because he works all hours, Dad expects his workers to work 24 hours a day too if necessary. I knew that would lead to conflict between us.

Instead, I opted for the easier task of making flat caps, earning £200 a week, training hard and partying hard with Lee. I left home to live with Lee at his mum and dad's house, and also kipped at other players' apartments sometimes; we had a great time. Apart from me and Lee, the workers on the factory floor were women and it took us a while to get used to the banter. I've heard plenty of changing room mickey-taking in my time, but these lasses could certainly dish it out and, to start with, we were both pretty embarrassed at the things they shouted at us. They were rum old buggers, some of them, but after a while we got used to it and started to give it back. It was a fun place to work.

The whole experience was a great learning curve for me and I enjoyed working there, pressing material and going out delivering. But it all came to an end after about six months when I got accused of sleeping with the boss's missus. He called me in and said: 'I think you're having an affair with my wife.' I was taken aback. I said: 'I can tell you it's not true, but don't you think you ought to ask her?' But he just replied: 'I think it's better you leave.' So I said 'fair enough' and walked out. It wasn't fair but, to be honest, I wasn't too bothered. I was young and carefree and six months seems like a long time when you're that age.

Also, I know what it's like if a bloke gets that sort of demon inside his head and I knew it was better if I went. The hat factory had been great to me and Lee and the gaffer had given us flexibility to go off and train when the club needed us to. It had also helped fund a lot of partying, so it had served its purpose. Despite the fun, I was also training hard and, after leaving the factory, I started full-time at Salford. I knew I was impressing Greg and that I was nudging closer to making my debut.

But when the chance eventually came I was terrified. I was named on the bench for a game against Featherstone and all I could think of was 'I'm 17 and I don't know if I'm good enough.' I never even got on and was very relieved, which shows I wasn't ready for it. The whole experience was surreal and I even got drug-tested, even though I didn't play. But, looking back, it was really good for me and Andy Gregory knew exactly what he was doing by exposing me to the experience.

By the time I made my debut at 18, I was a lot more confident but, even then, it was still a lot to take in for a young kid. I don't think fans realise just how tough it can be for players making their debut. Mine came against Sheffield Eagles and I spent the whole of the warm-up feeling a little overwhelmed, looking at the crowd and worrying about how heavy my legs had suddenly got. As the years went on, it became an obvious sign that I was nervous if I got heavy-legged before games.

That first match went okay even though, a few minutes in, I needed nine stitches under my eye after Paul Broadbent accidentally dropped his elbow into my face. I was being stitched up by Chris Brookes, who is now the England and Wigan doctor, when a message came in from Greg: 'Where the fucking hell is Malc?', or words to that effect. I was a bit worried at the thought of annoying Greg, but Chris calmly sent a message back: 'He'll be out when I'm ready and not before.'

Anyway I got back on and I must have done alright because I got picked again the next week against Halifax - and had my first close-up experience of Karl Harrison, who later became my Salford and England coach. Playing against the likes of Karl was yet another reminder of the world I was now mixing in and underlined how hard I had to try. Karl had won and done most things in his career and I wanted some of that for myself.

In that 1997 season, I played about eight or nine games and some people will be shocked that I'd then got the nerve, on the strength of it, to go on my own and ask the club for a new contract. I still had another year left on my initial deal but knew that if I was in the first team, Salford should be paying me more than £2,500 a year, plus match fees.

Greg sat there with the chairman, John Wilkinson, and told me in no uncertain terms that, rather than give me an increase, he would put me on the transfer list and put me on so high that nobody would want to sign me. Most 18-year-olds would probably have been psyched-out by that, but I poker-faced them both and called their bluff, telling them to transfer list me if that's what they wanted. The look of shock on their faces was quite amusing and, a few minutes later, I walked out with a new £12,500 a year, two-year deal.

The following year, I was named captain against Halifax and became the youngest Salford skipper since Paul Groves. I captained the side a few more times that season, so back in I went to see Greg and the chairman. This time they knew they couldn't try and bluff me because, quite rightly, I pointed out that you didn't have to be Einstein to work out that the captain had to be worth more than £12,500 a year when some players in the team were on £100,000. This time I left with a £18,500 deal which, the following year, I negotiated up to £22,500. My next raise went up to £30,000 and the rest I'll keep private. But the point I'm making is that I always knew my worth and felt Salford should pay what was due.

Greg obviously knew the players would support me when he made me captain, even though a lot were far older and more experienced than me. Personally, I thought I got it before my time, but I matured into the job pretty quickly. I've always been a good talker, but never over-talk. There's no point in overkill; players only have a certain attention span before you've lost their interest.

I said earlier that the team was really supportive of me when I got the captaincy, but I know for a fact that I had previously been seen as a threat by one player in particular. We were on a night out in Leigh when our first choice hooker, Peter Edwards, came drunkenly over to me. He was blind drunk and had been sick on the floor, but he staggered over and warned me that I'd never get his shirt.

Peter had been a New Zealand international at full-back and he was super fit. But being the worse for wear, he said I was making him look stupid in training. Normally he's a really nice bloke, but I just looked at him and thought: 'I'm bloody well having your shirt whether you like it or not.' And I did. Peter was moved to full-back when I made my debut, but I'll never forget what he told me and I vowed never to make the same mistake. Peter was probably feeling the pressure because he was coming towards the end of his career, but he made me even more determined to take his place. By showing his concern, he made his position weaker. As I got older, I made sure I never let on to a younger player that I felt threatened at all.

Rob Parker

● Malc is one of my closest and most trusted friends and will be until the day I die. But when I first met him properly, when I signed for Salford in 2009, I would never have guessed that we would become such good mates. And that's because of the frosty way he treated me at first.

I obviously knew of Malc before I joined Salford, but I didn't know him as a person and couldn't work out why he seemed to be keeping himself away from me. I discovered later that Malc puts enormous importance on loyalty and he wanted to work out whether I could be trusted before he'd let his guard down.

Ian Sibbit did weights with Malc and apparently Sibs was telling him that I was one of the lads and that I was alright. But Malc is very astute and switched on about people. He wanted to reach his own conclusions and so, unbeknown to me, I was put to the test. Malc let slip something about somebody and then waited to see if I'd go blabbing about it. When I didn't, he knew he could trust me.

The Devil Within

He actually revealed I had passed his test when we went on Salford's infamous 2009 trip to Jacksonville. I was so surprised I almost expected to be invited into some kind of secret handshake gang. But it said a lot about Malc and we just clicked from then on. We still laugh now about how he put me into quarantine for three months. Sometimes I speak to Malc more than my wife. We trust each other completely and I have total and utter respect for him, not only as a player and a family man, but also for his morals and values.

Malc once had the opportunity to leave Salford and go to Australia to play in the NRL. That would have been massive for him and made his career. I know he now regrets not doing so, but it doesn't surprise me that he didn't because he wanted to stay loyal to Salford. This is a man who has the word 'loyalty' tattooed on his chest. He is quite literally Mr Salford. That's why it was such a major shock when the club released him and I know they hurt him badly. Malc would never dream of treating somebody like that.

To survive at the highest level of any sport, contact or not, you have to be extremely tough and mentally strong, and I have been fortunate enough to play with a lot of tough characters. But there are only a handful of players I would include in an elite group who are that bit more special than everybody else - and Malc is definitely among them. Adrian Morley and Bernard Dwyer are two more. I don't know what it is about them; they have got something special, some sort of X-factor that makes them willing to die for the cause. Everyone has to be tough in rugby league, but people like those three will have my respect always.

That probably helps explain why Malc was chosen as Salford captain from the age of 19; he typifies everything that is right about a captain. He is a brilliant speaker in the changing rooms and knows what to say and when to say it. He knows when players need revving up or calming down.

Most importantly, Malc is a true leader. To use the analogy of war, leaders don't let their troops go out and die, they are on the front line too and fight to the death if necessary. On the playing field, you knew that Malc would be willing to die for his team-mates if he had to. Sometimes he didn't even have to say anything, he would just look you in the eye and you would be inspired to fight that bit harder. Respect is earned but also it's commanded and Malcolm did both.

Sometimes that bravery and his desire to lead his team out were too much for even his closest mates to understand. The week after Malc injured his neck - the injury that would end his career - he insisted on playing and I can remember him getting knocked unconscious when he dived on a ball, causing the nerves in his injured neck to impact massively on his vertabrae. It was actually my poor pass that he'd been trying to recover, but Malc was like a Jack Russell and would dive on anything. Anyway, the scans confirmed what he probably already knew, that he would have to quit... and still he refused! Malc insisted he wanted to play in the last game of the season in front of the Salford fans, even though he knew he might end up in a wheelchair. Shaun McRae, our coach, had a real tough job talking him out of it.

He might be crazy at times but he always led the players by example, even when he joined the coaching staff. In the 2011 pre-season, we went to an army camp north of Bury, where they used to film the TV series *Krypton Factor*. The Army lads tried to break us all weekend with the tasks they gave us and lack of sleep. One of the worst things was the 'Shitty Swamp'. It was covered in ice and when you jumped in, you went up to your nose. You then had to pull yourself along a rope for 20 metres. It was so toxic they told you not to breathe in; health and safety would have had a field day. Anyway, we were all in our skins pulling ourselves through when somebody shouted 'Team Us' to the watching coaches

- that was a quote we used, to show that everyone was in it together. Malc just went 'fuck it', stripped off completely and jumped in. He was covered in shit and must have been absolutely freezing but he did it, got out and announced 'Let's all do it again', even though we all knew he must have been crying inside. If he hadn't been naked I'd have given him a cuddle. But Malcolm show he was suffering? No chance! That's why every player respected him so much.

The hours he put into playing and coaching, and the effort he made to try and always be the best at both, were staggering. I have never met a bloke as passionate about the game as Malc. He would always go beyond the call of duty whatever he did and I know for a fact that he would be a successful head coach if given the chance.

Away from rugby, Malc is different again and a real softie with his kids. But I think that goes for a lot of blokes' blokes - they can be as hard as nails on the field but you often find that it's their families that really mean the world to them. Malc is exactly like that and in Sonia he's got the perfect partner. Somebody like Malc, emotional, determined and crazy, needs a tough character to keep him in line and Sonia is perfect at keeping him grounded. I know they've had their tough times, like everybody, but it's true what they say. Tough times don't last, but tough people do.

However, I can't finish without telling you about how notoriously tight with his money Malc is. Honestly, he gives stinginess a whole new meaning; the tightest man I have ever met. He's the type of man who would go for a night out with £40 in his pocket and return home with £50. I have no idea how he achieves it, although being the last to go to the bar and get his round in must have something to do with it.

I actually think that's the main reason he is mates with me; I always seem to be the one getting the drinks in. In fact, now I come to think about it, I'm actually bankrolling him.

7

*

Twickers in a Mist

I thought my life was working out pretty well when I became a first team regular and then got the even bigger honour of being made captain. But around that time it got even better and that was thanks to meeting the woman who I've been proud to call my wife for the last nine years.

I was injured one weekend and couldn't play so I was moping around a bit at the Willows watching the lads and wishing I could be out there too. But my mood improved instantly when I spotted Phil Warren with his missus Clare and a gorgeous blonde who I'd never seen before. Turned out Sonia was a mate of Phil's wife who knew nothing about rugby league and had no idea who I was.

We got chatting and straight away I liked her. We hadn't been talking long when I whispered to Phil that I was going to marry her one day. I'd always been a Jack the Lad and had never had a long-term girlfriend before. I liked to play the field. But I just knew that Sonia was the one I wanted to settle down with.

It sounds soft but that's just the way it was - not that I came over as a romantic. More like a twat, actually. We'd arranged a joint-date with Phil, Clare, Lee Hudson and his missus, and I was nervous because I wanted to impress Sonia so much. But God knows what she saw in me because - and I cringe about it now - I put an ice cube down her top and said: 'There, that's broken the ice, hasn't it?' It's not a chat-up line I'd normally recommend; you're likely to get a slap in most cases. But for some reason Sonia laughed and seemed genuinely to think it was funny.

Anyway, she can't have been angry because we ended up in bed together that night. Not that anything happened, to my disappointment, as Sonia insisted she wasn't the type of girl to have sex on the first night. But sex or not, I was completely hooked. And that's not always a good thing with me; I do become a bit obsessive if I really want something.

I was completely besotted and showed it. I guess I came over too intense too quickly for her liking and she fired me off a couple of months later after an embarrassing night out together. Not that I blame her. We'd gone to Andy Burgess's testimonial do at a hotel in Manchester and I was completely plastered. I desperately wanted the toilet but couldn't be bothered finding the gents, and so decided to have a pee against the foyer window outside. As I couldn't see through the glass, I didn't think people could see out - how wrong I was. There I stood, happily holding my cock in full view of everyone inside. Sonia was embarrassed and angry, not surprisingly, and the following day I woke up on my own, moaning: 'Bollocks, now I've blown it with her.'

We didn't see each other for a while but then our paths crossed again at a pub in Bolton. I've always maintained that she deliberately came looking for me because she'd realised what she was missing, but for some reason she has always denied that and claims it was purely accidental. As if! She can deny it all she likes, but not long afterwards I asked her to marry me and she said yes.

It wasn't the most romantic proposal in the world; I just blurted it out as we watched TV one night at her sister's. I had been thinking about asking her but maybe I could have put a bit more thought into it. I hadn't said anything to her mum and dad, but when we told them they seemed really happy. They joked that she was hard work and they were happy to get her off their hands. I say joked but maybe I should have quizzed them a bit more because, boy, can Sonia be feisty!

She's thrown a few things at me in my time and smashed a hole in the door once when she threw a pint pot at me and missed. Mind you, I know I've given her plenty of cause and, to be honest, I can't believe how lucky I am that she's stuck by me like she has. We've gone through a lot together but we're stronger than ever and that shows how great Sonia is. Not that she always seems like that of course. Like the time I woke up underneath a pile of pee-stained clothes. How was I to know that I'd been so drunk I'd pissed in the wardrobe?

Another night, Sonia wasn't best pleased when I woke her up and asked if she could speak to the taxi driver I was with. My problem, I slurred, was that I couldn't remember where I lived and could she please give him our address? I'm surprised she didn't give him a bogus one instead!

You might not believe it, but Sonia did actually have a calming effect on my drinking. Before we met I was down the pub three or four nights a week and a normal night's session would be about fifteen pints. My motto back then was: 'There's no point going out if you're not going to get blind drunk' and I stuck to that religiously, I can tell you. But I wasn't nearly so bad when I was out with Sonia. Suddenly, I was having fun being with her instead of necking pints.

It's when I'm not with Sonia that the trouble tends to happen. Like the time I went to the 2006 Challenge Cup Final at Twickenham... by accident. It was my testimonial season and I had a race night in Monton to which a lot of the lads came. It was a great night and I got chatting to a businessman who'd organised a trip to London, leaving early the next morning. He wondered if I fancied going and, hell, I thought, why not? Well, actually, a good reason not to go was that I was in charge of our son Mason, who was two at the time, while Sonia was in Italy at her best friend's wedding. But at 3.00am, as I waved my new pal goodbye for a few hours before we met again for the coach to leave for Twickers, that didn't seem to matter.

I knew my mum, who'd babysat Mason during the race night, would be cool about having him for the weekend. Sonia however was a different problem, but one I blocked out of my pissed brain as we set off on the coach and started getting bladdered again. As we approached Twickenham I remembered that maybe I should tell Sonia of the change of plan and so I phoned her.

'Is it okay if I go to Twickenham with some of the lads?' I asked.

'Well no, not really, seeing as how you are supposed to be looking after Mason and the dog,' she answered.

I could maybe have been able to sweet talk her if she hadn't then heard a lot of raucous noise from the other blokes on the coach and immediately demanded to know where I was. 'Actually, I'm near Twickenham,' I said. 'You fucking bastard,' she replied. Trying to regain some ground I told her I would get the train back if she really wanted me to, but she said: 'Well, you're there now so don't bother' and slammed the phone down. Result! 'Thank you,' I said, even though she couldn't hear me, and got back to drinking.

We carried on pretty much non-stop and before we had

even got to the stadium I was pissed. Everyone else got off the coach, apart from me and our Melvin. We decided we weren't all that bothered about a final between Huddersfield and St Helens; we'd rather keep drinking like maniacs. After another bottle of vodka and some Red Bull, the driver rang up the bloke who had organised the trip and we were told it wasn't a good idea for us to have any more on the bus.

Miserable sod, we thought, and got off for a walk-about with the fans, who were arriving in their thousands. I had a bottle of red wine in one hand and was signing autographs with the other. I can't have looked a pretty sight. But it got worse! Nipping back to the coach I spotted a luminous jacket and instantly decided that the best idea I'd ever had would be to strip off, put it on and start directing coaches into the car park. There's me, a Super League player and captain, pissed as a rat and telling buses where to go in my underpants!

I never did get to see the match and by Sunday I'd had enough booze to put most people in hospital. Sonia phoned me in the afternoon and asked where I was. Trying to get back in her good books, I said: 'Back home'. That seemed to calm her down a bit but it didn't last long. She ended up getting back from Italy before me and when I finally turned up I was blind drunk again.

I eventually made it home that night in a taxi and fell flat on my face on the lawn in front of a very angry Sonia. My dad and Melvin got me into the house and the next morning I had to get up for a full conditioning session. I dragged myself to the bathroom and reeled in horror when I saw what was in the mirror: a full face of make-up, painted-on moustache and eyelashes.

That night after training, me and Sonia had one of our famous 'silent teas' where neither of us spoke. But, after a day or two, Sonia had forgiven me and we even had a laugh about the whole episode. Another silent tea followed a disastrous trip we had to my parent's caravan in Wales one weekend. I was being rested and, as I wasn't playing, Dad suggested that me and Sonia join him and Mum there and I could be in a fishing competition that he was taking part in.

Dad ended up winning and so we all headed out to the boozer that night in good spirits. But, as usual, I ended up so drunk that I got gobby and argumentative when Sonia said she'd had enough and wanted to go back to the caravan. We argued so much on the walk back that Sonia locked me out, which just made me even angrier. I started punching the door and shouting for Sonia to let me in, but she was having none of it. I ended up hitting the door so hard I managed to punch my way through the aluminium and forced my way inside. And that's why being so drunk is stupid. Anybody sober would have known that I wasn't helping the situation by wrecking the caravan.

Sonia was livid with me by this stage, so I stormed off and was gone so long that she and Mum and Dad started to get worried and set up a search party. Eventually, they found me comatose in the storage section of the awning, so they left me to sleep it off and hoped I would be in some sort of shape to go to Sonia's nephew's christening the next day.

With a silent truce hanging over us, me and Sonia were on our way there when I got a call from Karl Harrison, our coach at the time, to say that Chris Charles has pulled out ill; he needed me to play. Play? I could hardly stand up straight and stunk like a brewery! As soon as I arrived, all the lads could see that I was massively hung over and there were a few ripe comments about how badly I smelt. But Karl didn't say a word and couldn't really, seeing as I'd been given the weekend off. The daft thing is, although I was rough as toast, I actually played pretty well. Oh yes, and to cap it all, that was the weekend Mason was conceived.

8

*

Running the Gauntlet

Gareth Hock is the highest profile rugby league player to be caught using cocaine. He copped a two-year ban after testing positive in 2009. But, believe me, he's certainly not in a small minority. Lots of players either take or have taken the drug. And I should know because I used to be one of them.

It's another confession that doesn't sit easily with my conscience; I know I was an idiot for risking my career. But it's a society problem, not just a rugby league problem, and wherever you get young adults nowadays there's a fair bet that cocaine isn't too far away if you want it. It's a massive social issue; people would be very naïve to think that rugby players don't come across the stuff regularly. Many succumb to its evils, or pleasures, depending on your point of view.

For me, cocaine was neither evil or pleasure. It was just something I did when I was too pissed to make any sense of anything and it always left me wracked with guilt after. Yet, occasionally, when I got hammered again and was at a party where it was being handed around as openly as drinks and food, I would foolishly do it again. And so end up back on the cycle of self-loathing.

I hold my head in shame thinking about it, but although I took it quite a lot, I was never an addict. Usually it coincided with two or three-day benders when my reasoning was clouded by alcohol. It's an old school belief that everybody snorts a long line of it; I guess you only do that if you're a massive user and need a lot and often. When I did it, you'd put a little bit on a coin and take it like that.

I first took cocaine in my early twenties. In those days a player could get tested during the week, so you can imagine the worry players went through when they sobered up and realised they still had cocaine in their system - it can hang around for up to five days before no longer being detectable in a drugs test.

I always had a big fear that I would get caught and did all the things people claim will get rid of it faster; sweating it out in a sauna, drinking lots of water, loads of Vitamin C. That might be rubbish advice but I would try the lot because I was so scared that my name would be called out for testing when I wasn't clean. In his book, the former Aussie great Andrew Johns called it 'running the gauntlet' and I know exactly what he means. It was agony, surviving those few days after you'd taken cocaine, knowing that your whole life could come crashing down around you at any moment.

And the thing is, it was never ever worth it. I got very little from it and cocaine is certainly not what it's made out to be by a lot of users. It sobered me up, if anything, and made me think more clearly - but by then the damage was done and I was already on my guilt trip.

Nowadays the World Anti-Doping Agency tests for cocaine only in competition - ie 12 hours before and 12 hours after a game. But to my mind that's pretty pointless. Most players wouldn't dream of taking it so close to a game. You'd have to be pretty stupid to run that sort of risk although, as we've seen, some players clearly are. But most aren't, so maybe they should bring back testing in midweek, several days before the matches take place.

The other downfall about testing so close to games is that cocaine isn't sport enhancing, so players wouldn't usually take it near a game anyway because it does nothing to make you play better. At the moment they've got the testing the wrong way round, in the wrong part of the sporting week.

Gareth Hock's high-profile ban shows the drug testing can obviously work. But the system used to be fraught with weaknesses, such as in the early days when the testers used to be waiting at training for players to arrive - wearing 'drug tester' badges that you could see a mile off. I've known players who've spotted the testers and shot off because they knew they might test positive. They then changed the system so that the testers would pounce after players had started training so it was harder for people to escape - but I've still known it to happen.

As I said, I've taken cocaine more often than I like to admit, but I haven't touched it since I got the bollocking of my life off Sonia. And to this day, I have no idea why I even admitted it; I never did it when she was around because I know how completely anti-drugs she is. It was about six years ago. We were in our new house and I was painting the walls and everything was nice and cosy between us as we tried to lick our new home into some sort of shape. Maybe the paint fumes had got to me, I don't know, but my conscience suddenly pricked me and I decided to confess. I certainly must have been having a weird moment because, if I'd stopped for even the slightest second and thought about it, I'd have kept my trap shut.

Sonia went absolutely ballistic, in fact off-the-wall

ballistic. She went mental, shouting and behaving like a raging bull, and left me in no doubt about what she thought of me. I was standing there with a paint brush in my hand, thinking 'Bollocks, why have I gone and told her?' It's not as if I'd even taken it for a while. But, for some reason, I'd had the urge to get it off my chest. The following day I met some mates and said: 'You'll never guess what I did last night.' They couldn't believe I'd been so stupid. They were calling me a dickhead and all sorts.

I was certainly left to regret the sudden confession because Sonia's rant didn't just last for days. She was so annoyed that she kept throwing in a few barbed comments for the best part of a year. But at least now I can go to my coffin and know I don't have any secrets from her. Mind you, I wasn't thinking that deeply at the time. I was just thinking what a prat I was for blurting it out!

9

*

Betting against Salford

While I'm baring my soul, now is probably the time to talk about betting against my own team, Salford. Sean Long and Martin Gleeson are still probably remembered, unfairly, more for their own betting shame than for all the medals they won between them in their illustrious careers. Longy infamously copped a three-month ban, and Gleeson a four-month suspension, for betting on their own team, St Helens, to lose to Bradford by more than nine points in 2004.

They each put on £1,000 and won £900, but they also ended up getting hit in the pocket by £7,500 fines. And so, if those two got caught and paid for it so expensively, why did I think it was worth the risk later on to do a similar thing? Well, for one thing, I wasn't as daft as those two and would never have dreamt of putting on the bets in my own name. And, unlike Gleeson who actually played in that game against the Bulls, I was never part of the Salford line-up when I did occasionally bet on us to lose.

The Devil Within

I can remember at the time Longy and Gleeson got banned, the RFL's chairman Richard Lewis said that there was no evidence that 'betting against the rules of rugby league is a widespread problem.' Well, I can tell you this, it might not be a problem as such, but it's far more widespread than Lewis would have you believe. It would actually be a surprise if it wasn't.

As long as you are not playing in a game you are betting on and therefore cannot influence the result, it isn't really frowned on by most players I know. If you've got inside information and can get somebody else to put the bet on for you, then I don't see that it's a problem. It's only a matter of knowing how strong or weak your team is, ahead of most other people, and if you've got that sort of information then there is possibly money to be made. You are not willing your team to lose - you are just being realistic.

If you bet on a horse, nine times out of ten it's because of a tip someone has given you, often somebody with inside information from the stable. In rugby league, it is exactly the same situation and I'm certainly not saying this because I was coining in the money. Quite the opposite - I won the first time I did it and then lost on the next four or five bets, so I decided I was a pretty useless gambler (even with my so-called inside info) and packed it in.

I never played in the games I bet on and only decided to gamble in the first place because me and a few other senior players were out injured so I didn't think we'd win. I can't even remember who we played against - that's how small a deal it was at the time - but I put on £400 and won about half of that back. I knew it was against RFL rules but couldn't see the harm in it.

As I wasn't injured very often in my career, my chances to bet on Salford's results didn't come up very often. But on each of the few times I tried again, I lost money and anyway betting has never really bothered me. I didn't have a lot of money that I was prepared to gamble with and my life is too busy to be bothered with studying form and so on. And I have always believed, whether it's drinking or gambling, that you should only spend what you can afford.

Whenever I bet against us and the wager didn't come in, I was always genuinely pleased that the lads had done better than I expected. If I'd have been gambling money I couldn't afford to lose, then I'm sure I would have felt more gutted. Some fans may think I was being disloyal, but I honestly don't think I was. I only ever did it when I was injured and, if I was fit to play, I can say hand on heart that I have always been the ultimate professional.

Quite a few players like betting on games but, truthfully, I have never heard of anyone other than Gleeson who bet on their own team to lose a game they were playing in. Everybody I know would think it immoral to try and engineer a defeat for their own team and mates.

Blokes being blokes, they always think they know better than the bookies, mind. And even I, who can take or leave gambling, am sometimes convinced that I can spot a dead certainty. A case in point was early in 2011 when I was still on the coaching staff at Salford. Steve Simms did our game-plan for a match after Shaun McRae left. It might as well have been written in Chinese for all the sense it made to me and, I suspect, the lads who were being asked to follow it. That whole week's build-up was a comedy of errors in my view and it looked like a gameplan destined to fail. A betting man would have put stacks of money on us losing. But I'll state loud and clear that I never contemplated doing that; I was involved as the assistant coach. I was convinced that the team was heading for a fall, though.

And that match, for me, summed up the stupidity of gambling. Because, against all the odds, the players went out and won. Admittedly, they ignored Simms's gameplan, but it just goes to show that there's never such a thing as a certainty in sport.

With one exception! Or so I thought a few years back, when I heard that a bookmaker was offering odds on which side would kick off in certain designated Super League games. That isn't, in itself, so easy to predict - unless, of course, you have two captains who agree it between themselves beforehand.

I'd heard that had happened and decided I would have some of that. I planned to approach the captain of one of our forthcoming opponents, who I thought would play ball. But, just my luck, the little scam was ended before I got the chance. The bookies spotted a lot of unusual betting being done on kick-offs, sniffed a rat, and abandoned the bet.

10

*

Mad Monday Mayhem

'Fuck off Tinkerbell, you've not won,' shouted the bingo announcer. The entire pub burst out laughing and I (the Tinkerbell in question) had to slink back to my chair rather embarrassed.

My pink tutu and ballet top only added to the amusement in the Merrie England boozer in Blackpool, one of the many watering holes on our 2009 Mad Monday. But then there's no shame when it comes to fancy dress outfits on the traditional drinking mayhem that signals the end of every rugby league season.

But I was still convinced I'd won the bingo. All the lads had decided to join in and the bloke on the mic had told everyone that the winner had to sprint to the stage as fast as they could. I wrongly thought it was me, hence my lightning quick ballet dance, but didn't realise the game was rigged so everybody would win at the same time. As you can imagine, when that happened it was chaos. But it was nowhere near the carnage caused by Rob Parker at the end of the night.

The Devil Within

We were all smashed and none more so than Rob, who was in his first year at Salford. I went to the toilet and there he was, having a pee, but with his kecks around his ankles. He was swaying all over the place and didn't have a clue what was happening, so I pissed in his underpants and he didn't even realise, even when he pulled his trousers back up. As we walked back to our table, Rob literally had piss dripping out of his trousers. He slurred: 'God, I must be really, really drunk... I've just wet meself.' Everybody fell about laughing when I told them. Even Rob thought it was funny, which goes to show just how blathered he was.

The end of every season throws up similar tales because the players feel as if they've been let loose. All year, they are like hamsters going round in a wheel of training and playing and then comes Mad Monday. Freedom. All the pressures of trying to win and keep hold of your shirt are released and that's why you do go way over the top sometimes.

When I started out, Mad Monday used to take place on the Monday after the final game, but now they start right after your last match and carry on until the last player runs out of steam. If you play on a Friday, you will inevitably be destroyed by the Tuesday, when it finally fizzles out.

Coaches like John Harvey and Karl Harrison used to come on Mad Mondays, but just for that day. I liked that because it kept the players under tighter control and it is important that players and coaching staff are seen to celebrate together after going through the entire season. But Shaun McRae refused to go on them when he arrived at the club, and he also stopped the rest of the coaching staff from joining in as he didn't want the responsibility if things got out of control. I thought that was wrong. If a coach is asking a player to go to extremes for him during the season, then it's only right that you should all be part of things at the end as well; it shows togetherness and mutual respect.

But Shaun was adamant he wouldn't come and, without the beady eye of the coach on us, that's when things started to go haywire. At Salford, team celebrations took place at the Willows, where we always had strippers. One year, Stephen Myler - now playing rugby union at Northampton - had an experience he won't want reminding of. One of the strippers called him up to the stage and covered his bare backside in whipped cream while we all cheered and clapped. At this point, Stephen seemed to be quite enjoying himself until she called for one of us to go up and whip him. I didn't need to be asked twice. I raced up, took the whip and absolutely leathered his arse. Stephen was howling like a maniac and a fight nearly broke out between us, I'd hit him so hard. I thought it was pretty funny, but I must admit I was shocked when he turned up for pre-season training several weeks later and still had the weal marks on his backside.

On another occasion, one of the lads who I'm not going to name because he's married with kids, ended up naked and on all fours as one of the strippers tried to have sex with him with a strap-on. We were all looking on, and even some of us were a little shocked, but the player just kept shouting out for her to give it to him.

Karl Long - Sean's brother - was also there that night for some reason and Karl can be a bit of a handful at the best of times. But with a belly full of beer and strippers on hand, Karl surpassed even his own wild antics. Having been to the toilet, he came crashing back through the door at full pelt straight into one of the performers, who he blindsided and tackled to the floor. I honestly thought he'd killed her, he hit her with such force, and she went down with a right bang. But, good on the lass, she staggered back to her feet and got on with her act.

If you think this was all getting a bit out of hand then you're not wrong. We were all pretty wired and it got a bit too ruthless; there were some boisterous lads at Salford then. But we reckoned without one pillock cocking things up completely. The lad in question was blind drunk and decided it would be a great idea to go into the car park, get in his car and drive at high speed, one-handed, doing hand-brake turns while drinking ale with his other hand. When he ran out of beer, he abandoned the car, came in for more and then went out and started the whole crazy routine again.

We, of course, thought it was hilarious. As you do when you've drunk your own body weight in ale. Two people who didn't find it so funny, though, were Salford chairman John Wilkinson's wife and daughter, who just happened to call in at the club at that time and copped a mouthful of abuse from our mad motorist on one of his journeys to and from the car. Not surprisingly, the chairman was told and two days later I was hauled in, as captain, to see him in the boardroom. He let me know in no uncertain terms that the behaviour was not befitting of the club and that, from then on, we were banned from staging Mad Monday at the Willows.

I took it on the chin, knowing full well that things had got silly. What I couldn't take, though, was the sight of Salford's Football Director Steve Simms sitting in on the disciplinary meeting. After all, Simms had appeared to enjoy himself at one of our Mad Mondays in the past. That was the year when he warned us to delete any photos we might have taken of him when we all returned to pre-season training.

Prior to our ban from the Willows, we also had another experience that no doubt lives long in the memory of some unfortunate grieving mourners! The naked run is a tradition at every club, where players who fail to score all season are made to run around the pitch in the nude as punishment.

At Salford it was a little different. We had the Captain's Run and I always loved to take part, even though I never went through a season without a try to my name. I must admit I'm quite happy to get my kit off when I've had a few, so the run was always great fun. We lark about the entire way round, tackling each other, and then do a mass naked wrestling session under the posts at the end.

This particular year, Luke Robinson had brought a large dog's mascot head to wear, so one of the lads was wearing that as we ran around the pitch. I'd also heavily tackled Jason Flower, forgetting that he'd only just had a shoulder operation, so you can imagine we were a pretty daft sight by the time we made it around the field to the Tavern, where we were greeted by all the other lads throwing beer over us.

And that's when we noticed there were a lot of people staring, open-mouthed, out of the Tavern windows. Turned out they were a funeral party and this was not the low-key sombre atmosphere they had been expecting to find. Not that it stopped us, I have to say. We moved out of sight, but then decided to send Shaun McRae something to remind him of the fun he was missing out on. Shaun had a saying about walking a plank and then raising it six feet and how much more difficult that was. Swilling with beer, we decided to test his theory - in the nude.

We balanced a plank from the railings to a big bin, and I walked across it while Karl Long held my testicles and Ian Sibbit video-ed it on his camera so that we could send it to Shaun. The next day, I had my season debrief with Shaun and, as expected, he took it really well. Shaun can always take a joke, so we were pretty certain that me balancing on a bar with my bare balls being held by Karl would raise a laugh. In fact it was the main topic of conversation.

Mind you, Mad Mondays don't always end up as tales of belly laughs and lairy behaviour. I can vouch for that after getting a whopping black eye off a stripper! No matter what people may imagine when they hear of players being let off the training leash, Mad Mondays are not about trying to cop off and cheat on their partners. They are about celebrating the season together after everything you've been through. And that's why I flipped one year when a stripper followed us after we left the Willows to carry on in Manchester. She obviously fancied getting laid by a rugby player, but I told her in no uncertain terms that she wasn't wanted. I must admit I gave her more verbal abuse than I should have and she clearly didn't like me calling her the devil. But thinking she had got the message, I went to the toilet and assumed that was the end of it. Wrong! As I came out she caught me cold with a direct punch. It was a decent hit and I knew it was going to be a shiner, so I called her a bitch and pushed her over. The doormen came rushing over, told her they'd seen her punch me and chucked her out. The other lads thought it was hilarious and I got quite a bit of stick about getting a black eye off a woman. I then copped a bit more off Sonia, who told me I deserved it.

Another year, I ended up with my entire face blacked out, although it took me a few hours to realise why people had been looking at me strangely all night. That year's fancy dress theme was superheroes so I went as Superman, but I didn't have any hairspray to get the quiff right. I phoned our Melvin and he had some black hairspray he said I could use. Being Melvin, I should really have sussed that everything was not as it seemed but, being the trusting type, I sprayed it all over and didn't think anything else about it until later that night in a club, when I started sweating and my eyes began to sting. I went to look in the toilet mirror and a black face stared back. My brother had given me black car bumper spray. Anyway, the night was still young so I just wiped my eyes and carried on drinking. It took me days to get it out.

Fancy dress is always a great source of amusement and one year we went to Blackpool, me in a huge cow outfit complete with udders and big ears, and our Melvin in a cowboy outfit that had an inflatable horse attached. The only trouble was he couldn't get the horse to inflate, so the entire weekend he had to drag around this limp, heavy mess.

While we were there we met the Warrington players who were also on their Mad Monday and Martin Gleeson was in a right state. We decided to abduct him for the Salford team and, on the Sunday, a load of us went back to Wigan, where Martin lived, to carry on drinking there. By this time Melvin had swapped his cowboy outfit, and limp horse, for a male stripper outfit that had a big inflatable knob on it.

It was a right laugh going round Wigan and that night we crashed at Martin's apartment, only to wake up at 7am with a start and realise we'd only got an hour in which to get back to Salford for the start of Mad Monday proper. I was still dressed as a cow and Melvin as a stripper and when we went outside to hail a taxi we couldn't spot one anywhere. We decided to go back in and ring one from there, because neither of us had a mobile. But we were now locked out and there was no way Martin was going to wake up, no matter how loudly we knocked on his door.

Eventually, we found a phone booth and that must have looked odd with a cow and a stripper squashed inside, but we still couldn't manage to get a taxi. Maybe word had gone around that there were two lunatics on the loose. I knew it wouldn't look good if we were late, so we raced to find an open shop. When we finally did, although they were pretty shocked by the sight of us, they called a cab and we were only a few minutes late for it all to start over again.

Your choice of fancy dress can play a big part in your day, as our prop Gareth Haggerty once found out to his cost. All the players turned up as golfers, as agreed, but for some reason Gareth came as a giant chicken. You can imagine the stir that caused among little kids in Blackpool - he spent the entire day being pestered by kids who wanted him to pose for a photo with them. They thought he was a giant friendly mascot rather than a bloke intent on getting legless.

But he stuck it out and the next day was still wearing it at Blackpool station as we waited for the train home. I was about 20 metres away when I yelled at him to run at me. Gaz is as daft as they come, so he set off with his wings flapping, huge webbed feet stomping away, and charged straight over the top of me. The platform was packed and you could see people wondering why a giant chicken had just run over an innocent bystander.

Another year Ian Sibbit went in a wheelchair, dressed as Andy from the sketch in *Little Britain*. He was in a real state when Melvin started pushing him fast along the cobbles in Manchester and tipped him out on to the ground. Sibs was so drunk he couldn't get up, but I'm sure a lot of passers-by thought he was genuinely in a wheelchair and that his wicked carer had had enough of him.

In my last Mad Monday at Salford we all went to Terry Newton's pub dressed as geeks, where he put on a good spread. Terry wasn't drinking, he was working the bar, but he had a good laugh with us all the same. For most of us, that would be the last time we would ever see him.

11

*

Feeling like a Zombie

The flip side to all this insanity and drunkeness is, of course, the sanity and professionalism of training endlessly, sometimes to the point where you think you'll never be able to put one foot in front of the other. For all my tales of drinking, and I admit that booze has played a big part in my life, there are also times that people never see - Christmas Days when I'd be out pounding the streets on my own, or nights at home when I'd rarely touch a drop.

Although I've sometimes gone crazy when out drinking, I can also be a picture of sobriety that would suprise a few. And, as well as my professional pride, the one constant that keeps me sane and grounded is Sonia and the children. You honestly can't beat going home to your family and spending quiet quality time with them.

I always wanted kids, right from being young, and as soon as I married Sonia in 2002, I was keen to start a family. Sonia didn't want to rush into it, but by the time she got pregnant midway through the following year she was just as happy at the prospect as I was. We were both thrilled at the thought of welcoming a new little Alker into our lives. But we didn't expect it to be me, and not Sonia, who was rushed into hospital first.

Sonia was overdue when I began to get pretty brutal stomach pains that wouldn't ease no matter what. At first I thought it was trapped wind, so I did sit-ups and press-ups to try and relieve it, but the pain got worse and worse and, in the middle of the night, I couldn't stand it any longer. I woke Sonia up to say I'd better go to hospital. I was given morphine and, the next day, my appendix burst and dripped into my hip, meaning I had to have that drained as well. It was all very painful and I was out of it at times, but all I could think about was Sonia at home on her own, heavily pregnant and, by this stage, several days overdue.

I was in hospital for four days and every hour I expected to get a message saying that Sonia had been admitted after having gone into labour. Nothing would have stopped me getting to her, morphine drip, burst appendix or anything, but luckily I was released before she finally did go in, nearly two weeks late.

I've always considered myself mature when it comes to planning for my future and, even from a young age, I had my head screwed on with regard to finances and trying to provide for my family. But becoming a dad was something different altogether. I admit that I found the birth completely overwhelming. Sonia did superbly throughout, whereas I was there crying my eyes out at the sight of our beautiful new son. We were absolutely overjoyed and I immediately went into protect mode as I realised that I'd now got this helpless little baby to take care of. And boy was it a swift and difficult learning curve. Neither I nor Sonia had realised just how exhausting parenthood would be.

Mason had a lot of mucus problems, so we hardly slept

for the first two weeks of his life. We'd have to take it in turns to tip him upside down at regular intervals to help him get rid of all the black horrible stuff that was troubling him so much. During this time, I also went back to training and played my first game eleven days after my appendix operation. I shouldn't have done that because I'd been told to have six weeks off, but I was fired up with the need to provide for my new son and the only way I knew how to do that was to keep earning my living as a rugby league player. It was a ridiculous thing to do. I lost a lot of weight as a result and didn't recover fully for a long time.

I was like a zombie for much of those early weeks, due to Mason's health problems, my recent operation and training way before I should have. And there was no chance of going out drinking to wet the baby's head. I had a quiet drink with my mate Karl Fitzpatrick and that was it; I just didn't have the energy for a big session.

Weeks stretched into months and me and Sonia were still half awake as it turned out that our gorgeous little baby was also very hyperactive. He wouldn't sleep during the day and wanted attention all the time. When Sonia went back to work, her sister looked after Mason while I trained and then I'd pick him up and face the task of entertaining him while trying to do up our new house at the same time. It badly needed work, but it was exhausting doing that and keeping one eye on Mason at the same time. Life was a 100 mile-per-hour rollercoaster and it sure had an effect on my energy levels and matchday performance.

But, you know what, I wouldn't have changed a thing because Mason was everything I had always wanted. Five years later, our baby girl Madison arrived and this time it was Sonia who cried at the birth, she was so happy we'd now got a daughter and a son. I found both births very emotional and it's certainly true when they say that kids turn your world completely upside down - for the better. Becoming a dad made me face my responsibilities. And although I've still done plenty of stupid things since they've been born, I also know that I'd go to the end of the earth if necessary for my kids and Sonia.

Before I had children, I would get really down if I wasn't playing and desperately miss the hustle and bustle of being involved, plus the craic of being with the lads every day. But when you've got kids you don't have the time to wallow in those sort of feelings, there's too much to do at home.

I guess I'm two extremes. Fans know me as this hard case on the pitch; other people will see me as a bit of a nutcase off it, when I've got a drink in hand. But most people didn't see me as the dad who always insisted on pushing the pram and changing nappies when the kids were babies. I've always been very hands-on with the children and Mason had a soft rugby ball in his hands before he could walk or crawl. I used to think he would become a rugby player because he could spin the ball with both hands before he was three. We were always passing a ball to each other. But when he went to school it was football that got him hooked.

But while I couldn't have been happier as a parent, what used to make me a happier player did, at one point, become quite a complex routine. I've said before that I can get quite obsessive and that trait definitely showed up in my pre-match rituals and superstitions. I would lay all my clothes out in the spare room the night before, in exactly the same position and 'right' order. When they were laid out correctly I'd say a prayer, holding the rosary beads and a medal that my great grandmother had given me shortly before she died. I loved my great gran and can still remember the days I'd go round to her house and she'd pour us both a Guinness as we watched the snooker - I was six or seven at the time.

With my prayer over, I would then leave the room and

wouldn't allow myself to go back in until the following day. That was fine unless I forgot something and then it would drive me mad. One day, I'd forgotten to lay out my deodorant and knew it would upset my entire routine if I put it there the next day. I had to ring Paul Highton and ask if I could use some of his instead. It really got that mad, but I couldn't help myself. I was locked into this superstitious ritual that couldn't be broken.

I used to wear the same lucky underpants for games from about the age of 16 until I was well into my twenties. They had that many holes by the end that my crown jewels weren't even covered, but I was convinced that my game would be affected if I didn't have them on. I also had a waterproof jacket that I trained in over winter and refused to wash. It got so stiff I could stand it up in the corner of the room and it wouldn't collapse. It must have stunk to high heaven, but I convinced myself that any smells would disappear whenever it rained.

I'm not alone in having routines, but they can get quite time consuming and awkward if you go away with the team and are sharing a room. I always tried to make sure that my routines didn't impact on the people I shared with, but I would sometimes find it uncomfortable trying to say my prayer if somebody else was watching.

Other players aren't as considerate and I've known some who have put their own routines ahead of their room-mates. I think that's wrong; ultimately it's the team that counts most. For example, we stayed over on one trip to Harlequins in 2010 when two of our forwards, Ray Cashmere and the current Salford captain Stephen Wild, were sharing. Ray locked Stephen out of the room for two hours because he wanted to sleep, but that left Stephen having to wander about when he maybe also wanted to rest. Ray could well have had a blinder when the game came, but there's no point in one player doing well if others are knackered and the team then loses.

Although I tried to accommodate other players, I admit I've always been happier being able to follow my own routines in my own way. I guess I'm a bit OCD in a lot of things I do. If you came into my office at home, it would probably amuse a lot of people to see how all the different envelopes are lined up in exactly the right positions.

My wardrobe is also a shrine to tidiness and order. The hangers have to hang in the same direction, with pants at one end, then non-collared shirts, then collared shirts and Sonia knows better than to put anything away for me. I need to make sure everything is just so.

I don't know where this all came from but I can't help myself. I even have a stapler in my van so that I can clip petrol receipts together as soon as I get them, to avoid them getting messy and out of order. And when I started to work regularly in the building trade, my accountant used to laugh because she'd never seen a builder who was so neat and organised. She even told me to stop being so meticulous, because it wasn't necessary. I bet there are not many builders she's had to say that to.

After I started on the coaching staff at Salford early in 2011, the lads would give me stick when it came to my video review sessions. I couldn't start until I had various sheets of paper with all the information laid out neatly on the table, so that I knew what order to discuss things in.

Sonia is used to all this of course, even the fact that I like to do our food shopping (pushing prams and now pushing shopping trolleys... my hard man image is disappearing by the minute). But I do enjoy it and can happily spend hours food shopping and spending too much money in Asda. I took over the cooking responsibilities at home more to keep Sonia away from it than anything. We'd just moved in together and Sonia cooked a really nice shepherd's pie, which I complimented her on. So we had it every night for two weeks. I was soon becoming sick of it and suggested that maybe I should take over. I've done the cooking ever since, but we don't have shepherd's pie very often.

With Sonia and the kids at the Willows -
Having children doesn't half change your priorities!

Shaun McRae

● The best way for me to sum up Malcolm is to give you a war analogy and paint a picture of what it must be like to be crouching in a bunker, waiting to go over the top into battle.

Quite rightly, many people might be scared that injury and possibly even death await those brave enough to charge forward, especially in the front wave. But not Malcolm. If the call went up for someone to be first out - knowing they might not make it - Malcolm would be that man. It would take a fair bit for the enemy to knock him over and I reckon there'd be a good chance of him actually getting to where he wanted to go.

And if the same scenario presented itself the next day, you would get exactly the same result. Malcolm wouldn't sit back thinking 'I led them out yesterday, it's someone else's turn now', he would be first out of the bunker again. And if, by some freak chance, Malcolm didn't make it, then you could bet that every single one of the men behind him would be talking about what a good bloke he was.

The Devil Within

Before I became Salford coach I'd only met Malcolm a couple of times at awards dinners, where he was picking up his almost obligatory Top Tackler award. I didn't know him well. I knew, of course, that he had a reputation for being an exceedingly strong, tough player who was a tremendous leader and it didn't take long for me to realise that he thoroughly deserved that reputation. Straight away it was obvious that he commanded a lot of respect from everyone at Salford, particularly his peer group. But it also quickly became obvious that Malcolm wanted to keep learning and adding to his knowledge and ability. We soon forged a very good working relationship that became a close friendship which still exists now, even though our paths have taken us in different directions.

Malcolm had that talent many leaders possess - the ability to turn the switch from having fun to being deadly serious and professional. Malcolm likes a laugh and can be funny (sometimes when he doesn't actually mean to be) but he can then turn very quickly. I've known a lot of players who, once they get into that silly, jovial behaviour cannot then get out of it quickly and you can't get them to focus or concentrate again. But Malcolm, like every great leader I've known, could suddenly sum up a situation and go straight to being totally focussed on the job that needed doing.

So for leadership skills, Malcolm rates exceedingly highly. But when it comes to physical and mental toughness I would have to say that he's got to be one of the toughest players, if not THE toughest, that I've ever worked with. On the surface, it appeared like you just could not break him physically or mentally; no matter how hard you pushed him he would come back wanting more. Maybe he went home after some sessions and was in agony, but he would never let anybody know he was suffering. Obsessive isn't the right word, but his toughness was certainly something he played on. He always wanted to be the hardest and most competitive and that was a great example to the other players, particularly the younger ones. Malcolm gave blood, sweat and tears in every single session.

The collisons and tackles in rugby league can have an horrific effect on players' bodies and, as you get older, it takes more time to recover. Sometimes, in his later playing years, Malcolm would come in and he couldn't turn his head because of his neck injury, but he would never put his hand up and ask to miss out anything. I had to encourage Malcolm to understand the logic and strategy of him maybe missing certain sessions and Malcolm would always listen to advice and he'd understand the reasons. You could never force Malcolm to do something, but he would always listen to reason and was constantly wanting to learn everything he could. His longevity in the game speaks volumes.

As a coach I always believed in players having a say and expressing themselves and coming up with ideas; Malcolm loved all that. To say he was hard-working and dedicated is an understatement, although he did get a surprise at the workload he was expected to do when he came on to the coaching staff. Players often have no idea of the work that's involved behind the scenes before a training session and the work that then carries on after they've all gone home, and Malcolm was one of them. So when he joined the coaching staff he was surprised but, in typical Malcolm style, he threw himself into the work and put in some really long hours because he was determined to do a good job.

Many players struggle with the emotional side of things when they have finished playing and go into coaching - especially if, like Malcolm, they stay at the same club where they have played. Suddenly they go from being one of the lads to someone who has to be slightly detached. It's tricky balancing the act of staying friendly with players you've been close to and then being able to dish out criticism. But he handled all that very well. He still had a good rapport with the players and was able to show he could have the authority that coaches need.

Sadly, as we all know, Malcolm's career at Salford ended suddenly and traumatically and he admits he struggled to cope. I wasn't at the club then because I was still trying to recover from a stress related illness myself, but when I spoke to Malcolm I realised that he was posssibly heading the same way I had and I didn't want that to happen. I told him that I didn't want to get involved in the politics of what may or may not have happened and I wasn't going to judge anybody, but I was keen for him to know that I was there for him if he wanted to talk. Because I'd gone through similar pressures and stresses, I was able to help him cope and get things off his chest. I'm glad to say that I managed to help him. But that's what friends should do - friendships should endure everything.

Now, thankfully, Malcolm is back to his best and doing well with his building business. But I'd really like to see him back in rugby league and that doesn't necessarily mean in coaching, although Malcolm would make a terrific coach if someone gave him a chance. There are so many other things he could offer the game in terms of mentoring or in an ambassadorial role and it would be a real shame if the game passed up this chance to get Malcolm involved. I really hope he uses this break to take stock of where he is, reflect on things and decide what he wants to do with his life. And I really hope that means he comes back to rugby league in some way.

To sum Malcolm up, I'd simply say he was one of the toughest and hardest players I've ever worked with - but one who was a sheer pleasure, on and off the field.

12

*

The Pain Game

I began this book in a deliberately shocking way because I wanted to give readers an instant insight into the pressures all rugby league players face on a daily basis.

Many fans will look at us enviously if they are stuck in boring low-paid jobs and that's understandable. Players, if they have any sense, know they are lucky to be doing a job kids dream of. And I bet that, almost to a man, no player would give it up voluntarily. But it's certainly not the easy, dream lifestyle you may think.

I heard that Jon Wilkin and England U21 and stand-in football manager Stuart Pearce both spoke to VIP guests at the 2011 Challenge Cup final between Wigan and Leeds at Wembley, and their comments summed up perfectly the thinking behind this chapter. St Helens and England forward Wilkin described the mentality of rugby league players going through the pain barrier, desperately trying not to show on the outside that they are hurting, even if they might be in agony on the inside. Straight-talking Pearce gave his view of the different approach taken by football players, saying: 'Week in, week out, I look at players trying to convince us they are hurt on the outside when we know on the inside they are not.'

And it's because of that bravery shown by rugby league players that the sport has a very big problem - and one that could blow up in its face if the powers-that-be don't address the issue soon. Make no mistake, there have already been instances about which the sporting public has been kept in the dark. I am convinced someone will get killed if nothing is done. It is that serious.

The root of the problem is rugby league players' reliance on painkillers, because they are taught from an early age that it's not the done thing to show any hint of weakness or pain. My first encounter with them came when I was about 25 and I'd torn my abductor in training, a few days before a match. I was in so much agony that I knew there was no way I'd be able to play that weekend and so resigned myself to missing out. But the following day, after a scan confirmed I'd got a tear, the Salford physio gave me two Tramadol tablets.

I had no idea what they were, but Paul Highton said he took them and I was happy to give them a go if they would help to ease the pain. From there began my slow slide into becoming one of rugby league's many painkiller junkies. Within hours I felt loads better, not 100 per cent, but the pain had eased to a level where I thought I might be able to play after all. Convinced I'd been given a miracle cure, I took two more on the Saturday and got through training without too much discomfort. I told coach Karl Harrison that I felt good enough to play on the Sunday and, before the match, took two more tablets. I could still feel the injury, but nothing compared to the pain I'd had the day after I'd done it, and I managed about 50 minutes before Karl took me off. I was stunned that I'd played that long. Three days earlier I could hardly move without wincing.

Of course, those tablets hadn't actually cured the injury, they had simply masked the pain. I badly wanted to believe that Tramadol was a miracle cure, but any sane person could have told me the reality. But that's the problem; players don't want reality. They are under so much pressure to perform that if a perfectly legal drug is going to help them there's no way in the world most players would not hold out their hand.

After that first amazing result, I took them intermittently for the next several years until it got to the point, later in my career, where I was taking them all the time. I had slowly but surely convinced myself that I couldn't operate without them and doubt I would have got through the last two years of my career had that not been the case.

Every player will do whatever he can to play and, I'll stress again, taking Tramadol is perfectly legal. But hand-in-hand with it, very often, come sleeping tablets because it's a drug that can also keep you awake. And when that happens, suddenly you can find yourself on a constant cycle of uppers and downers. To make matters worse, in rugby league there doesn't seem to be any brake on how many a player should take. And that's why so many, including myself, become totally reliant on them. Popping the pills becomes habit-forming.

In the end, whether I had niggles or aches and pains or not, I would take the Tramadol because I truly believed that if I didn't then I would be in pain. So what had started as a necessity gradually got to the stage where I was taking six a day out of apprehension. On top of that, there was the worry that if I stopped taking them I would face at least one of two problems: 1) the pain would come back and might stop me playing and 2) I'd have to face the hassles of coming down off the drugs. As I found out later, to my cost, going cold turkey really isn't that pleasant and I only did it because I'd reached the end of my tether. Contemplating doing it while you're still playing is a no-go area.

Many players fall into the trap and abuse the situation because they know tablets are handed out pretty freely by clubs. After one Super League game in 2011, 85 Tramadol and 69 Diazapan were given out. This is not an accusation, I'm simply saying that after games most dressing rooms can look like *Holby City* and lots of players genuinely do need painkillers to cope. They are quite often given strips of four or six Tramadol, but without any warning leaflets about side -effects that you'd get from your local GP. As you've initially got them from the club medical staff, you automatically trust them without question. Why wouldn't you?

And once you realise the benefits to be had, you want more. At times in my career, I was in so much pain after matches that Sonia had to help dress me the following day so I could get to training. She'd help put my socks on and the like. Then I'd hobble downstairs and take my Tramadol and, hey presto, I was ready to go again. You don't care that the tablets are only hiding the problem, the all-important thing is showing you are fit enough to be part of the team.

Of course, players do get reminders that these tablets are not the miracle cure many of them would wish for, but few take much notice. Once, I had a dead leg, but there was no way I was going to go in and see the physio with something like that, not when I had my magic pills. I convinced myself the painkillers would sort it out. But whereas some physio treatment and a couple of days rest would have solved the problem, I ended up being out longer than I should have.

Mention of the physio brings me on to the many varied reasons why players are under so much pressure to hide their injuries. These are pressures that all players will have felt at various stages in their careers, such as:

1) Players simply do not want to be seen in the physio's room. It sounds ridiculous when they are trained to such a high level, but that's the way I was brought up by my family and the coaches I had, like Karl Harrison and Jimmy Lowes. Team-mates would see you as soft if you went to the physio too often and Karl and Jimmy would class you as 'energy sappers' on the team. You couldn't avoid it if you had a big injury, but I would never go in with a niggle even if I knew the physio could sort it out. I'd rather take the Tramadol. And so begins the never-ending cycle.

2) You need to train to get picked and if you are injured you cannot train. If the painkillers get you onto the training pitch, you're going to take them because every player knows that his position will be taken by somebody else if he can't play. If your replacement does well then you could be facing several weeks on the sideline, when your injury had only required a one-match lay-off. From my third contract, I was never on appearance money as I always managed to negotiate a decent deal, but some players at Salford were on £400 or £500 a match on top of their normal pay, so the pressure to stay in the team, for them, was even greater. Players on appearance money are desperate to play, whatever injury they have. It's an extra few hundred quid with which to feed their family.

3) Fears over not getting a contract. We've all been there as players, even the best ones. The only way you will get another decent deal is if you are selected regularly and playing well. That can put enormous pressure on a player if he's worried his club might get rid of him. And if you are a worrier, like me, it can have an adverse effect on your performances. Just when you desperately need to play well, you can find yourself in the awful position of doing just the opposite. Imagine if you're not even in the first team and you've got those worries. How do you face your wife and

kids and tell them that you might not be getting another contract? I would bet that, at any one time, more than half the players at the majority of clubs will be on painkillers on a regular basis. Most don't think about the consequences of becoming reliant on them because their first priority is to provide for their family.

4) Internal and external pressure to be the best. As well as the contract pressures, there is also the pressure players put on themselves to be the best, plus the pressure the club puts on them to perform. If the club doesn't do well, then that can obviously have a knock-on effect on income and finances - and therefore down the line a squeeze on the players' own contracts. Fans only see the 80 minutes of game time each week, but I can tell you that players go through loads of other personal lows and highs. For instance, can you imagine what it's like sitting in the team meeting and your name isn't called out in the 19 for the next game? You know you've 'failed' and your team-mates know it too. It can be a lonely place in the dressing rooms at times.

5. Being captain. As the captain I always felt it was my responsibility to be the best in every training session. Even if I was in the world's worst mood, I never allowed myself to turn up for training sulking or down. One person's misery can rub off on the rest of the team and you don't need that. Quite often I'd have a false smile on my face at the club, but that pressure builds up and inevitably your family cops the full blast of your temper once you get home. Also, even though I was captain, I never once had the mentality that my selection was automatic and probably put undue pressure on myself as I was always worried I might not get picked. The way I coped was by taking Tramadol.

6. At the back end of my career I started to find it hard to keep up with some of the younger guys. For 12 years or so I had always been at the front in everything in training and I

Above: Me and our Melvin in Scott Lane, Wigan, in the early 1980s
Left: Majorca, 1980. Me with a wrong-shaped ball! I was born in 1978.

Left: Me, Michael and Melvin at Salford Quays in 1989. How posh we were

Below: Me in my first year at high school in 1989, looking rather weird if you ask me

Above: My dad, also called Malc, in Portugal, 1986...
...and with mum, Jacqueline, at Wigan's old Robin Park

Left: Four brothers - me, Melvin, Michael and Marlon at Blackpool, 1993

Below left: Me and Melvin get ready for Santa, 1987

Above: The Alker brothers with Dad in the Waterside pub, Billinge, in 1990, when he played for Wigan St Pats

Left: Me and Melvin at Brixham, 1990

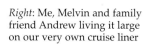

Right: Me, Melvin and family friend Andrew living it large on our very own cruise liner

Above: Me with the Academy league winners trophy in 1996

Above: In action for Salford - week by week, I gave them everything I had

Right: National anthem time with England 'A' in 2005

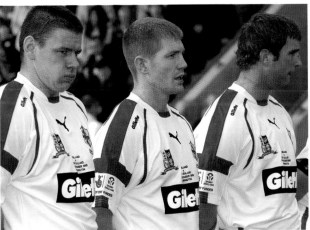

Above: Luke Swain, myself and Rob Parker - all for one and one for all!

Left and below right: I was well known for my defence, but there was far more to my game than that - I wasn't a bad distributor of the ball too!

Left: James Roby feels the force as I make my way up the tackle count

Above and left: Playing is only part of the modern-day player's job. There are media duties to contend with - and I always threw myself one hundred per cent into training, whether I was injured or not

Below: An upside of relegation - the following year we won the Northern Ford Premiership

Above: Sonia, me and Dad about to enter a fishing competition at Sandy Bay, Wales, in 2003 - which we won. *Above right*: Enjoying some outdoor peace and quiet

Above: Dad and me with that very same fishing comp trophy in 2003

Left: Sonia and me on our wedding day, 2002

Below left: Mason and me celebrate the 2008 NL Grand Final victory

Below right: Presenting an award to my brother Marlon at Wigan St Pats

Left: I made a lot of good mates at the Willows. Here's me with Stuart Littler, Ian Sibbit, Karl Fitzpatrick

Right: ...and celebrating our 2008 Northern Rail Cup win with the one and only Craig Stapleton

Right: Good rugby league mates such as Iestyn Harris, Karl Harrison, Jamie Moore and referee Ian Smith come together for a questions and answers night in aid of my testimonial

Above: Mason and Malcolm Alker join the Power Rangers at Disney World, 2008

Right: The Alkers hold the Northern Rail Cup

Below: With the Northern Rail Cup in 2008

Above: An emotional end to my playing days at Salford, as I pose for one last time on the pitch with my children, Mason and Madison, in 2010

loved it. The buzz of training hard and being the best was incredible. But in the latter stages I was having to push my body harder and harder to stay at the front and something eventually had to crack. In the end, just about everything cracked. In those last two years I was on six Tramadol a day, sometimes more, just to try and prove myself in training.

7. When I went on to the coaching staff at Salford my money dropped substantially, which is only to be expected. I was also only given a one-year deal, so yet again I was locked into this permanent worry about my future and how I'd support my family. It's a never-ending concern, whether you are a player or a coach.

Many readers may have some sympathy by now, but a lot will take the opinion that players reap what they sow and I suppose they do have a point. In any walk of life, people take risks to maintain their standard of living or their jobs. But the difference here is that players are gambling with their health - and worse, their own and other people's lives. I believe that the game is turning a blind eye to this, because it's a problem that is so hard to solve, given that painkillers are prescription and not illegal drugs.

It may sound preposterous to claim that rugby league players' legal drug taking is a risk for the general public, but consider this. How many are driving their cars when they are under the influence? I did it quite often when I clearly wasn't in a state to drive and I know several others who have too, some going so far as to crash their car.

After I finished at Salford, when I had plunged into depression and gone off the rails, I drove my own car partly onto the pavement because I was so spaced out on sleeping pills and Diazapan. I smashed my tyre after careering up the kerb and just thank God that there weren't any pedestrians about at the time. I didn't have a spare, so I drove for fifteen minutes to find a garage and by that time there was nothing left of the tyre I'd smashed. That's how stupid drugs are. They make you think you can do things you are clearly not fit to do.

Diazapan is a muscle relaxant whereas Tramadol is a painkiller, but mix any of them together - or with sleeping pills - and it could become a lethal cocktail. You feel relaxed and chilled out. Some people can feel drowsy and that's no way to get behind the wheel of a car, yet you have no idea your judgement is impaired. If this goes on, someone will either kill themselves or someone else.

On top of this, there is alcohol. Most players don't think twice about drinking even though they are already taking more drugs than they should be. I was lucky in that I could always train with it all in my system, although that did give me a false sense of security and I ended up abusing my body more than most.

Other players didn't have that resistance. Sometimes, at Salford, we had players who were so under the influence they couldn't catch a ball in training to save their lives. One day, when I was on the coaching staff, one particular player dropped a ball three times in succession and Shaun McRae sent him home to get his head sorted. Shaun didn't know he was spaced out on drugs, he just thought he was hung over. But I know of other clubs who have been aware of what's going on and yet, to my knowledge, not followed it up with any lectures or advice about the dangers.

Salford did attempt to ban sleeping tablets after the 2010 Super League Magic Weekend in Edinburgh, when a young player got absolutely spaced out on pills and booze and ended up making an idiot of himself in the hotel foyer. But it's tough to stop their use. Players can easily find them and do. No drugs are impossible to get if you know where to go.

I've also known players who used Diazapan as an excuse if they turned up to training drunk or hung over, so drugs can be used as a cop-out at times. And if the clubs are handing them out to help players cope with injury, then they can hardly turn around and complain when they are 'accidentally' combined with too much alcohol.

The combination of sleepers and booze can be lethal but, after games, many players take sleeping pills to help them get over the adrenaline of playing, any energy drinks they may have consumed and possibly the Tramadol. If you've had a night match, you can still be sky high by 11.00pm and yet know you need enough sleep to get up fresh for training the following day. Yet come the next morning, the reality is, lots of players can't remember anything they said or did the previous night. I believe it would be best for clubs to give players the day off after a game, but most prefer to get them in, to try and prevent them from going on benders. Quite often, I've been in video review sessions where players were fast asleep. One of the worst for nodding off was Craig Stapleton, who would have his head back, mouth open and snore like a chainsaw. Nobody woke him. Even coach Shaun McRae was cool about it. Mind you, Craig does have five kids, so he had a good excuse.

I've heard of clubs trying to prevent young players from taking Tramadol, but they can easily acquire them off other players, who get them from various sources as well as their own clubs. Can you imagine the suffering of players who get hooked as teenagers? Thankfully, Tramadol over-use is now starting to get noticed as a problem in society at large, and I gather GPs have tightened up the rules as to who can be prescribed them. But nowadays you can buy them easily off the internet. I never did so, but I know lots of players who have ordered them from companies in countries like Romania, with no guarantees about how pure the drugs may be. Players order thousands at a time, no questions asked. Some companies ask for a prescription to be sent to them AFTER they've delivered the drugs to you and nothing is done if a prescription isn't sent, as is usually the case. It's madness, but that's why the Tramadol problem is so hard to sort out - and probably why nothing serious has so far been attempted.

But something desperately needs to be done and the RFL needs to start educating players and club staff alike because I'm sure many people don't understand the long or short-term side-effects. Also, clubs need to be made more aware of the pressures players feel they are under to take these drugs. Players certainly don't take them for any sort of high; they take them because of the pressure to train and play and put food on their family's table. Before they know it, they are addicts.

The Rugby Football League has a duty of care to get to the bottom of this problem and I would gladly give them my advice. After all, I've got a lot of experience to draw on. But I'll hold my hand up and admit that I don't have a ready-made answer. You cannot ban painkillers because they are a necessity in a collision sport. If you stopped the use of painkillers, you would lose half your players every week.

But it's a problem that does need addressing, that's for sure, because it's already spiralling out of control. Maybe one solution would be to make sure that Tramadol is only taken for specific pain over a short period and to ban it on gameday, with a test brought in to make sure that players aren't then going out and using the drugs from sources other than their club. Players could also be asked to sign some sort of exemption form. Currently players with asthma have to declare what medication they are on; maybe a system like that needs to be initiated.

Don't get me wrong, I'm not saying that painkillers are wrong in themselves. They can help people, especially in a tough sport like ours. When used properly, these drugs have a vital role to play. But sometimes players abuse the system and can't see through the mist because so many people in their circle do it and they feel their livelihoods depend on it. I played an entire season needing a shoulder reconstruction thanks to Tramadol and, by the end of the year, the doctor said my shoulder was hanging by a thread. Other players will go to similar lengths. Is that fair on their welfare and health? Maybe someone should step in and save them from themselves and their bravery.

I see ex-players who can't walk or move properly thanks to what they've put their body through for rugby league. It's really sad to see that some cannot even work after their rugby careers because they are so knackered. For some, it's down to normal injuries and wear and tear. But for others, it all began in the medicine cabinet.

The Willows wasn't the most luxurious venue -
but for one reason or another I couldn't quite leave it

13

*

Barrett's Home

I've always tried to be a really positive person and believe you should attempt to make the best of whatever comes your way. But looking back, I strongly believe I made two big mistakes in my career by staying so loyal to Salford.

Loyalty is so important to me I've got it tattooed on my chest. But sadly, at Salford, loyalty turned out to be a one-way street. If I'd known then what I know now about how I was eventually treated by the club, I'd have left when I had the chance. A couple of major offers came my way and, after thinking long and hard, I turned both of them down. What mistakes they turned out to be.

The first chance to leave Salford came at the end of the 2002 season, when we got relegated after six years in Super League. Bradford knew Jimmy Lowes was coming to the end of his career and they wanted me to join them as his understudy, with a view to taking over when he retired. I met coach Brian Noble and he explained that I wouldn't be first choice until Jimmy packed in, but I wasn't happy with that idea. It was naïve of me, but I told him I wanted to be the main hooker at a club and Salford would guarantee me that. When they heard about Bradford's interest, they began to promise me the world and gave me an offer I found too good to turn down.

Although my money would drop a lot for the following season in Division One, they also put a new Super League contract on the table for the following year if we got straight back up. The money they were offering if we were promoted would more than make up for anything lost in the meantime. That plus my insistence on being first-choice hooker made me decide to stay. It was a big gamble because there was no guarantee that we'd get promoted straight away, but it paid off. Long term, though, it's a decision I really regret. I'd been too stubborn to play second fiddle to Jimmy, but it would have been the best thing for my career.

I would have learnt a lot from one of the best hookers our country has ever produced, while joining Bradford would also have had an enormous impact on my future earnings. On top of that, playing for a team as good as Bradford were at the time would have helped win me the illustrious career at international level I'd always dreamed of. It's also a fair bet that playing for Bradford would have prolonged my career. If you're winning most weeks then that's a hell of a lot better than getting the hammer I was getting in a losing team. My body would not have been as broken as it was by the time I had to finish.

As well as my stubbornness over being the main hooker, much of my decision to stay at Salford was also due to that aforementioned loyalty. Chairman John Wilkinson pulled at my heart strings at the time, saying I should stay faithful to them because they had always been loyal to me. Knowing the personality that I am, he probably knew that would have an effect. But come the end, such loyalty didn't mean much.

Nowadays, I still reckon that loyalty is important when it comes to family and friends. But in business, it's bullshit. And it has backfired on Salford because other players have seen how they treated me at the finish and some haven't been inclined to make the same mistakes I did.

Yet even knowing all that, I still let myself fall into the same trap at the end of 2006. It was then that I got a call out of the blue to go play in the NRL in Australia. The future Huddersfield Giants coach Nathan Brown was boss of St George-Illawarra at the time and he wanted to offer me a two-year deal. It was a huge pat on the back being head-hunted by someone like that, but it was not an easy decision to make. I did want to test myself in the best competition in the world, but started adding up the reasons why it would be better to stay.

1) Salford had promised me a big money-spinning game against Warrington at the beginning of 2007, to complete the testimonial year I'd had in 2006.

2) I'd just bought a new house that needed renovating. Admittedly that was never going to be the factor that would stop me going, but it was a consideration.

3) Sonia wasn't keen on moving to the other side of the world at first, although she slowly came around to the idea. Still, I was worried how she and Mason would settle in, being so far away from our families.

4) Trent Barrett was delaying his announcement about whether or not he was leaving St George to join Wigan. My move depended on him going, to free up the club's finances, so it was a little unsettling, not knowing if it was definitely on or not. We were going to live in Barrett's house. To rub salt into the eventual wounds, I saw what it was like when I went on a working trip down under in 2010 - it was a massive beach-front property. A lot different to Salford I can tell you!

5) Salford gave me a deadline to sign the new contract they were offering me and were pushing for a decision.

6) I really wanted to taste some success with my current team, after being there for so long. We'd finished fifth in 2006 and I really believed that the following year we could push on and establish ourselves as one of the top four sides.

And so I turned down St George-Illawarra Dragons; the biggest mistake I've ever made in my life. First up came Salford's announcement that they had back-tracked on the promise to give me that Warrington match as my testimonial game. I was really pissed off about that because I should have got them to put it in writing, but hadn't thought it necessary as I trusted them.

In fact, I would have missed out on a testimonial game altogether if Karl Harrison, our coach, hadn't sorted something for me. He got me a game against Wigan, who were coached by Brian Noble, so I still managed to earn a few bob, but that was no thanks to Salford. I was luckier than Paul Highton and Stuart Littler who were both there eleven years without getting a testimonial game. That is Salford all over. They'll pull at your heart strings when it suits them, but don't give you the same loyalty in return.

Although the club's behaviour hacked me off, I still thought that, over all, I'd made the right decision in turning down St George. But all that changed as the season went on and my high hopes of helping Salford become a big club blew up in our faces. How wrong I'd been to think we were on the verge of some success - we got relegated instead! As I sat there staring at the prospect of another year in the lower tier, I really couldn't believe what a fool I'd been.

As at Bradford four years before, if I'd gone to the NRL, I would have improved my international prospects and boosted my earning capacity. Everybody who comes back from the NRL seems to be able to earn loads more than before they went. Once again, loyalty had hit me hard in the pocket.

While I ruined those two chances, I'll also forever wonder what might have happened if I'd joined Leeds. I'd always admired the Rhinos, not only for what they did on the field but for the way they carry themselves off it as well. It's a club I'd always wanted to play for and, at one point, under Tony Smith, it looked like I may get a chance. But it came to nothing and I stayed at the Willows. Story of my life.

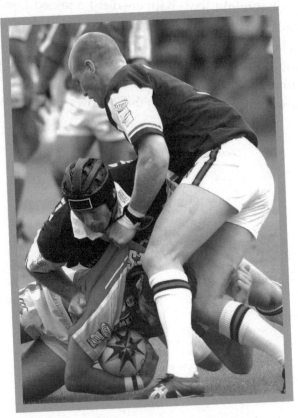

Mike Wainwright and me get stuck into London -
it seems I was destined never to play in Australia

14

*

Aussie Dreams

As I've said, it didn't take long for me to regret my decision to stay in England, but the enormity of it really hit me for six in late 2010.

Salford planned to send our conditioner Mike Eccles to Australia, to study how various NRL clubs organised their strength and conditioning set-ups. Our Aussie half-back Daniel Holdsworth told Director of Football Steve Simms that I would benefit enormously from the trip too, seeing as how I'd just had to retire and was now a full-time member of the City Reds' coaching staff.

I was grateful to Daniel for suggesting me and Steve agreed to the idea, to my delight. Although my relationship with Steve ended badly, he always used to champion my cause and Chairman John Wilkinson would tell me how highly he rated my chances of becoming a successful coach. It was a journey I was determined to learn as much as possible from, and it certainly opened my eyes to some of the differences between conditions and facilities at NRL clubs compared to Super League. It highlighted that Salford was a million miles off.

Me and Mike spent time at St George, Canberra, Gold Coast Titans, South Sydney and Cronulla, and we picked up tips and ideas from every single one of them. It also made me very envious of the facilities they regard as bog-standard - for instance, at Cronulla, they had a dozen staff just to set up the training fields ready for the players and coaching staff. At Salford that job was the responsibility of the head coach and his assistant. At times, I'd be on my knees getting to our training fields to set stuff out in readiness for the field session later. I was also amazed to see that the Aussies had three people just to set up water stations. This was light years away from carrying a massive water container on my own, on an eight-minute hike.

Everything about Cronulla impressed me, especially the way coach Shane Flanagan carried himself and helped us. He and the club went out of their way to share ideas and be helpful. Even when we got stuck for transport to get back to the train station, the groundsman offered to take us in his truck.

And Cronulla weren't on their own. All the clubs were friendly and offered us every possible piece of advice, me on the coaching side and Mike on conditioning. Coaches would talk openly about their structures, how they would isolate defences offensively, and so on. They didn't hang back with anything and that was great for my education. Sometimes you don't get that same openness in England and I think that's a little bit to do with us lacking confidence. Aussies are brought up with a winning, competitive mentality and maybe we need more faith in our own abilities. After all, there are no right and wrong ways to coach. It depends on your personnel and how you get the best out of them.

Me and Mike spent two weeks visiting the various clubs

and I felt we'd become pretty close during that time. But a few months later I got another harsh lesson in how you can't always trust people you once had faith in. I felt he let me down pretty badly when Salford pushed me out of the club and believe he didn't support me as I expected him to do. He was probably just trying to protect his own patch, but I would never have done that to a mate.

The trip did give me a chance to see one of my real pals, Craig Stapleton. He and his family really looked after us during the few days we spent at St George. As I mentioned, I never knew what I was missing when I turned down their offer, but boy did I soon understand what a cock-up I had made. 'Stapo' took me to see Trent Barrett's house in Shell Harbour and it was phenomenal, a dream. But the house was only a small part of the story. Everything made me realise how stupid I'd been - the clubs' professionalism, the state-of-the-art training facilities, the enormous high profile of rugby league itself. The different lifestyle may well have taken some time for me, Sonia and Mason to adapt to, but my game would have improved enormously in the NRL.

At some point in the future we may still go to live in Australia because I love the whole mind-set of the Aussies. One day, I went to the beach with 'Stapo' and his three sons and got a real taste of what it's like to live there. The boys were involved in a surfers club, which wasn't just about surfing but competitive games in general. One of them took part in a team sandcastle building competition which everybody took really seriously. That sums the Aussies up. The winning mentality instilled in them from an early age goes with them through to adulthood, whether in sport or industry. I don't think there's anything wrong with that. In Britain, competitiveness is almost frowned upon in some schools. But why should it be? For some kids, sport is the only thing they're good at, so why shouldn't we encourage them to be the best they possibly can be and let them revel in their glory if they win something? It's something I feel very passionately about and something the Aussies have got right. To look at their success in the international sporting arena is to know that the Aussies just love to win - and why not?

Also on the trip, we went to a strength and conditioning conference and I got speaking to a bloke who is heavily involved in weights and gym programmes at schools. From the age of 13, kids in Australia are taught technical aspects of weight training and so, even though they don't lift many weights, they are already being educated about its benefits and looking after their body. Most of the schools have their own huge, well-stocked gymnasiums. Most English people would struggle to think of anything comparable and that's such a shame.

Now I've given you a brief insight into the magnificent conditions and facilities at the NRL clubs, I'll paint a picture at the other extreme... The Willows. Yes, the changing rooms really were as bad as you imagined if you ever went to watch a match at Salford's uniquely ancient former home.

I always loved The Willows because it was a ground that oozed one hundred years of heartache and passion. It was a venue where supporters' hopes and disappointments were almost tangible and, to me, these sort of traditional grounds are what rugby league is all about. I'm not, however, saying that I loved the changing facilities because they really were awful. Up until 2011, both the home and away sheds had a massive sloping roof, due to the stand, so you literally couldn't stand upright in one half. It wasn't until a year after I got the captaincy that I finally got a peg on the left-hand side, where you could actually stand up. I never let go of it either. I didn't fancy going back to the terrible days of constantly banging my head on the ceiling.

As home players, we got used to the conditions, whereas the away teams all hated coming to the Willows. We always tried to make the most of that and make their experience as uncomfortable as possible. I really do believe that we got the edge on many teams in the early parts of games because their players were so wound up about how dreadful the changing rooms were.

The other weird thing about them was the position of the showers. You had to come out of the room and cross a corridor to get to them - all in full view of fans who were hanging about and reporters waiting for quotes. In later years at the Willows, they moved the press into a separate cabin and our changing room was also moved, so the cock-watchers lost out on their treat.

I proposed the decision to move our changing room after playing about on my computer at home, designing a new set-up further beneath the stand. I knew there was another room there that wasn't used for much, so I drew up designs, using that room and knocking through into the washing area, to create a much better and bigger changing room where everybody could stand upright. The club approved my idea and I even put in for the job of doing the structural work. But in the end I couldn't do it; I was away on my trip to Australia.

I was pretty chuffed with how it all worked out though, because it meant much better facilities for the players. That was what I always strived for, either as a captain or a coach. Nothing, of course, actually altered about the culture and, seeing as I've already mentioned cock-watchers, I'll let you into some of the secrets of our players and the merciless ribbing that goes on. When one lad joined us on loan, he was already pretty famous within Super League for being embarrassed at how enormous his dick is. We thought most blokes would have been pretty proud to have a massive cock and so wanted to judge its size for ourselves. So when he arrived we made him show us - and it was true, it was enormous. It was like a baby's arm, tripping people up.

Ray Cashmere also came in for some ruthless mickey-taking. He looked like a 1960s porn star when he took off his underpants. Not for the size of his knob, but the state of his pubes. They were out of control. We'd tell him he had to shave them, but he just kept firing back with the answer that his missus liked a real man. There are no secrets in a changing room and woe betide any bloke who's slightly out of the ordinary in any way.

Paul Highton

⬤ Malcolm's loyalty to his family and friends is legendary to anyone who knows him. But the thing that also stands out for me is how down to earth he is. No matter what Malc achieved in the game he was always exactly the same.

I can remember times at the club when we would have some pretty flash players and they would turn up in their Porsche Boxters, Mercedes and convertible Audis; then, around the corner, would come the unmistakable sound of Malc's old banger of a van. He would have his workman's hard hat on the dashboard and he'd get out all covered in mud, but he couldn't care less what people thought of him.

That was Malc to a tee on two counts. One, he didn't care how he looked and two, his van was the sign that Malc had probably already been grafting at his other job, as a builder and brickie for his own construction company, long before other players had even got out of bed.

That's the thing about Malc, when it comes to hard work he is an absolute machine. He was always the first at training and the last to leave and would work harder than anyone else at every single session. Even if all the lads had been out for a big night on the Friday and everybody was dying in training the next day, Malc would never show he was suffering. He might well have gone home and collapsed for all we knew, but he would never allow himself to show any sort of weakness to the other players in training or in games and that's why all the squad wanted to play for him.

I joined Salford from Halifax when I was 18, just at the time that Malc was breaking into the first team. We clicked straight away, even though our backgrounds could not have been further apart. I was an only child until I was 11 and I definitely wasn't streetwise, and so I'd be really shocked at some of the tales he would tell about him and his brothers. He was far more worldly wise and rougher and tougher than I could ever be, but we shared the same sort of humour and we've been firm mates ever since.

I also quickly realised that Malc would be honest and speak his mind no matter what the consequences might be. I'd only been at the club for a couple of weeks when I got the first glimpse of his natural leadership skills

Salford were on a losing streak and, one day, our coach Andy Gregory told us to go home, get our passports and pack an overnight bag because we were all going to Dublin. We were off to do something different, because training obviously wasn't working. Malc, who was 17 or 18 at the time, stood straight up and said he wasn't going because he couldn't afford it. He then told Greg that he didn't think he was being fair expecting him to pay.

Most of the other lads had probably been thinking the same, but they didn't say anything and I know for a fact they would have kept quiet and paid for the trip by extending their overdraft, or on a credit card, or by asking their missus to give them some money. But Malc had the guts to stand up and say what most of his team-mates were thinking. Greg left the room and a few minutes later came back. He told us that he'd spoken to the Chairman and the club had agreed to pay for the trip, if we all attended a sportsman's dinner on our return. The lads were all patting Malc on the back and calling him a legend because he'd got us a freebie.

That time Malc's outspokenness worked, but other times his mouth got him into trouble, because he always says exactly what he thinks. Some players would use that to their advantage, especially the Aussie players who may well have been opinionated but who didn't have the balls to complain to anyone in power. Instead they would give Malc the bullets and he would fire them. But because Malc always wanted the best for the players he would never shy away from the task, no matter how uncomfortable the discussions might be. He was not the type to avoid confrontation if he felt that something needed to be said on behalf of the team.

And that's partly why Malc made such a terrific captain. He would always back up his words with actions (unlike some skippers I've played for) and that's why he earned players' respect. Malc was young when he became captain and, at the time, we'd Martin Crompton and David Hulme in the side, who had both been captains during their careers and were both very outspoken characters. But they didn't faze Malc in the slightest. He'd speak his mind to any player, whoever they were. We also had some Aussies come over who had played the game to a very high standard and you could see them looking at Malc, thinking they'd never heard of him and that he was young. So they'd start off being a bit confrontational. Malc would immediately put them in their place and once the Aussies had seen how he trained and led by example, they knew he was a warrior and from then on he had their respect.

I'm not saying Malc's mouthy trait is always a good

thing though! And I should know after having many a night out with him that's ended up in a fight or trouble. Usually we slip into good cop, bad cop mode, with Malc getting us into trouble and me trying to calm things down and pulling Malc away when things look like they're getting out of hand. After a while, I got so good at reading the signs that I could head off trouble before it had even begun by getting Malc out of the way or by somehow diverting his attention.

I hadn't been out with him the night he had a massive fight with Jon Clarke and I can still remember him coming in the next day and telling this far-fetched tale about how his feet had come to be so badly injured. That was for other people's benefit, of course, but he'd always tell me the real story later. Anyway, despite his serious injuries, he still played that weekend. Most players would have been out for two weeks, but Malc never allowed himself an excuse not to play.

His drinking and fighting are legendary, of course, but I don't think that's any different from many players. The pressures of playing the game are so high, and the training so hard, that I think many lads see it as their reward to go out drinking and let off steam. Malc will be the first to admit that one drink is too many and ten not enough, because he's not the type to have a couple of quiet pints and then go home for tea. Once he starts it can go on for forty-eight hours. But, as a close mate, I also see him as the doting family man and the times when he'll go six months without a drink.

It's hard to sum Malc up because he's like two different people at times. He is one of the most colourful characters I have ever known away from the game, but when he switches into training or playing mode then he becomes the ultimate professional. He is Mr Salford, a legend at the club and quite rightly so. And if he'd been allowed to continue his coaching career there I'm also convinced that he'd have become one of the best coaches ever - let's just hope another club gives him a chance.

But I can't finish off all soppy and full of praise. Instead, I'll give you another insight into the weird workings of Malc's mind. He is famous among his team-mates for the wacky things he says. To Malc, they appear to make perfect sense, but to everybody else he can talk sheer nonsense at times. Like when he slapped Karl Harrison around the head as a joke and told him: 'Always expect the unacceptable.' Or the time he heard some of us talking about him at the other side of the pitch and shouted that he'd overheard, saying: 'I've got ears like a shithouse rat.' On neither occasion did he understand why everybody cracked up laughing. As I said, he's a legend, but a bloody daft one at times.

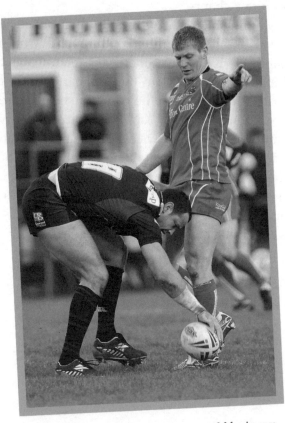

Adrian Morley - what a warrior - would be in my
Super League XIII every day of the week

15

*

My All-time Super League Dream Team

There have been some great players going the rounds since Super League first kicked off in 1996. Here are thirteen of the best, in my opinion.

FULL-BACK: KRIS RADLINSKI

Rads' support play was phenomenal. He was a great defender, very competitive and an all-round world class player. Off the field, too, he was a top bloke; very down to earth and not up himself at all. I really enjoyed watching him play and playing against him.

WINGERS: JASON ROBINSON and MARTIN OFFIAH

Jason was without a doubt the hardest person I ever had to tackle, he was so elusive. I never minded tackling anyone, no matter how big they were, but he was so hard to get hold of. He would side-step, duck, dive... you didn't know which way he was going. It was even worse when he returned a kick downfield, because the tacklers could get a bit isolated, and you could never guess the direction he was about to take. It was a massive loss to rugby league when he went to union, but money talks and that's sport.

Martin's pace and his finishing were a joy to watch, especially if you were in his side. He even kicked a drop goal for us once, in Salford's 50-1 defeat by Bradford (don't ask me what was going through his mind when he did that, I've absolutely no idea). Martin achieved so much in his career but there were no airs and graces about him. He got on with all the Salford lads when he played for us.

CENTRES: JAMIE LYON and MARTIN GLEESON

Where do you start with Jamie Lyon? He's got the lot. Jamie was a wingman's dream because he created an awful lot of space and would step and skip away. That one-handed pass of his, well, it was a thing of beauty. Wingers just had to be in the right place at the right time and Jamie would create tries for them. He was a pretty mean goal kicker as well.

I wasn't going to include Martin Gleeson at first because he plays on the right, like Jamie. But I decided he was too good to leave out. Glees was very similar to Jamie in lots of the things he did, particularly his off-loads, good footwork and the way he created one-on-one situations. He also shared that uncanny ability to send his winger in for tries.

STAND-OFF: SEAN LONG

Sean had everything a great half-back should. He was a very good organiser and kicker, a real tough lad and an excellent runner with the ball. He was also able to create a lot of space. A top class all-round player.

SCRUM-HALF: GAVIN CLINCH

This choice might surprise a few people, but because I was lucky enough to play with Gavin, I can appreciate just how good he was. He was the best organiser I have ever come across, with his talking and the way he moved the team around the field. His passing game wasn't particularly the best, but his organising and kicking game were top drawer. He would have achieved far more in a top four side, so that's why I've picked him next to Sean Long. The two of them would have made a brilliant half-back pairing.

I also fondly remember Gavin for one of the funnier moments on one of Salford's pre-season trips to Jacksonville, Florida. About seven or eight of us were playing a ridiculous drinking game where whoever lost had a cigarette stubbed out on their head by everybody else. I know it sounds mad but it was also funny, especially because Gavin became the target. He loved his hair and would dye it jet black, really proud of it he was. We engineered the game so that we'd all stub our cigs out on the same spot until he ended up with a bald patch. He was going berserk and Gavin is pretty amusing anyway when he's drunk, which made it even more hilarious.

PROPS: ADRIAN MORLEY and CRAIG STAPLETON

Adrian Morley - what a warrior! In every game he takes bangs, but he keeps on going and comes up with the big plays to get possession back for his team. He's big, strong, tough and the standard bearer. That's what you need from your props because they take the team forward and set the platform for the half-backs. Especially at international level, where games are so close and to-and-fro, you need your big front-rowers to keep putting their hands up for work and that's what Moz does all day long. And what a gentle giant he is off the pitch too. One of the nicest and most polite men I've ever met.

Craig Stapleton was a terrific competitor, great footwork, good aggression and tremendous at going forward with the ball. At Salford, he had a lot of pressure on his shoulders to take the whole team forward, but if he'd have been at a club like Wigan or Warrington, where the go-forward is shared amongst the front-runners, he'd have been outstanding. He wasn't able to shine at the Willows, which is a great shame.

HOOKER: JAMES ROBY

A machine, there's no other word for him. He's strong, a good tackler and an excellent runner with the ball, and is consistently a top all-round performer. It took him time to adapt to being St Helens' starting hooker after Keiron Cunningham retired because it's a different cardiovascular situation. But his engine has improved a lot since and I'm convinced he'll dominate that role for many years to come.

SECOND ROW: JAMIE JONES-BUCHANAN and GARETH ELLIS

Jamie Jones-Buchanan is a truly exceptional player with a massive heart who runs really hard and is always tough to play against. We were in England camp together a few years ago. Watching him close-up made me appreciate just what a all-round presence he is. Nothing's changed my mind since. The way he runs off the ball player is a real joy to watch and a massive attribute for any team to have.

Very few players have achieved what Gareth Ellis has managed with his successes in Super League and then even more eye-catching displays in the NRL. He had another top year in Australia in 2011 - winning West Tigers' Player of the Year award for an unprecedented third consecutive season - and has really matured as an athlete. His offensive and defensive qualities are second to none. For him to stand the test of time in Australia as he has done, shows just what a top class performer he continues to be. It's great that he has decided to come back to Super League with Hull in 2013.

LOOSE FORWARD: ANDY FARRELL

Faz was the complete player, the ultimate professional. He was a good kicker, strong in the tackle and could play numerous roles really well. I cannot praise him highly enough for how he played. A great loss to rugby league when he switched codes.

COACH: IAN MILLWARD

Basil coached the Lancashire team when I played for the county and I learnt an awful lot from him even in a short period of time. He has a lot of charisma and shows tremendous emotion and passion, but I think players need to see that. How can a coach expect his players to show passion if he's not showing any? Ian was technically very good and he is also a great man-manager and knew how to manipulate players to his advantage, even great ones like Andy Farrell. He could get the best out of players because he had that bit of fear factor about him, but he was also approachable.

You can't beat the feeling of winning some silverware

16

*

Coaches - Good and Bad

I had five main coaches in my time at Salford and learnt a lot from all of them - not all of it good! But I'd liked to think they would agree that they could always rely on me to come up with the goods (even if I was hung over).

My first coach, of course, was Andy Gregory and I'll forever be indebted to him for the opportunities he gave me. He signed me at the age of 16 from Wigan St Patricks and pushed me through far earlier and quicker than a lot of coaches would have been brave enough to do. Greg gave me the springboard to achieve by getting me training with the first team, long before I made my debut, and it was an invaluable lesson at that age to be working alongside and learning from guys like Andy Platt and Steve Hampson.

But, as you have already read, I certainly didn't get an easy ride. If anything, Greg pushed me harder than ever. He knew my dad from their Wigan St Pat days and because of that connection, I think, he felt he had to push me to my boundaries so that I'd show him what I was capable of.

You'll often hear coaches say young players aren't ready, but how do you know if you don't give them a chance? I think we lose a lot of talent in the game because of that mentality. But Greg was a shrewd personality and he knew how to encourage me. It was to my great advantage that I had a coach like him to start with.

Tactically, Greg was very good. He was a real players' coach who knew how to motivate us and what made us tick. At the end of the 1996 season, Salford got to the Division One Grand Final at Old Trafford. Even though I'd not yet played for the first team, Greg made sure I was part of the squad. We had suits made with the Salford emblem on the jacket and I'll never forget the thrill.

On the coach going to the stadium, they played a video of the highlights of the season and it was such a special feeling being part of that. The whole occasion was massive for me and as I walked round the pitch at the end with the lads - and the trophy - I knew I definitely wanted more of that. Not just as part of the non-playing squad, but as one of the starting line-up. Greg clearly knew what it would mean to me and it worked. I tried harder than ever after getting that taste of what it's like to win something important.

Greg had the guts to make me captain when I was only 19, even though I had only been playing properly for less than a year. It showed the faith he had in me, which says a lot, considering my age. But Greg knew I had the maturity to be captain.

It's no secret that Greg had his problems with drink, but for the biggest part of his career at Salford he had managed to keep them under wraps. But when he also started to have a few personal problems, it all began to get on top of him and the drinking became worse. It wasn't really a surprise when the club sacked him, but it was a shame. Sober, he was such a shrewd coach and businessman.

It's also sad that only people who are middle-aged or older will remember him as he should be remembered: a genius on the field, two-time winner of the Lance Todd Trophy and one of Great Britain's best ever players.

When Greg left the Willows, the Under-20s coach John Foran took over for a month. Then, for two years between June 1999 and July 2001, the Australian John Harvey took charge. John Foran certainly had some different ideas and he loved playing the dreadful song 'Bohemian Rhapsody' to us in the gym, making us do dumbbell shoulder presses in time to the music. As the tune got faster and faster we'd have to speed up. It didn't half look camp with us all prancing about, but John thought it was great. There's no way you could get players to do it nowadays.

The other trick he had with the younger guys was to insist on packing a load of weights onto the bar for bench presses. We'd look at them and say 'There's no way we can lift that boss' but he'd insist on us having a go. As we grunted he'd stand behind us, helping to lift the bar on the sly so that we thought we were doing it on our own. That was fine until you got to the first team squad and couldn't lift the weights you thought you'd been doing in the Under-20s.

John Harvey was an acquired taste. Not all the players liked him because he could be very blunt and if he didn't like or rate you as a player he'd tell you to your face. I've always preferred that approach, rather than the talking behind closed doors and back-stabbing you get from some people - and one person in particular at Salford! But not everybody could deal with John's brutal honesty and he rubbed people up the wrong way. I liked him, though. He was a good motivator.

One of the big problems John faced was that he wasn't given the facilities or materials he'd expected to get and his video review sessions ended up a joke. John only had a tape recorder to work with, which meant he spent most of the sessions re-winding and fast-forwarding to the bits of the game he wanted to talk to us about. Other club coaches at that time would have had computers and instant access to any bit of film they wanted to study, but poor old John was stuck in the dark ages at Salford with their equipment.

Where John did excel was his man-management skills with the players he rated. He was excellent at spotting whether you needed a break or not. Sometimes he'd look at me, realise I'd had a really tough couple of weeks working hard and actually order me home, with a warning not to return for a few days. Knowing my work ethic, he had to make sure I'd not be tempted back early by threatening to fine me if he saw me at the club. Under John, I was far fitter and fresher than I've been under any coach.

But there was one thing John hated, like most Aussies, and that was rain. You could guarantee that if it was raining at a training session John would take up position under a big tree next to the training ground and not come out again. All you could see of him was a puff of smoke from his cigarette and the giant coat he wore to go pig hunting back home in Australia. Occasionally you'd see him stick his arm out to see if it had stopped. If it hadn't, he'd wave his arm and shout for us to do one more lap.

John did struggle tactics-wise and he was probably out of his depth a little in Super League. Near the end of his spell in charge, you could tell he was getting more and more stressed because his head and face literally got redder and redder by the day. It wasn't a huge surprise when he was shown the door and Steve McCormack was given the job, which I was really pleased with because he is a great bloke.

Steve had been my Under-18s coach when I first got to the club and he made me captain. We used to travel to training together and I was convinced he was going to make a really good coach. He's since proved that he can be with the way he's turned Swinton's fortunes around, among other achievements. But back in 2001, I think his chance came a bit too early. We had a lot of senior players at the club like Bobbie Goulding and Warren Jowitt and he turned to them a lot for advice. There's nothing wrong with that as long as you still insist on doing things your way, but Steve lacked a bit of confidence in his own opinions and views on the game at the time. He got dominated a bit by some of the players.

But as a coach you've got to live and die by the sword and go your own way. If he'd been given another pre-season and been allowed to change a few players, bringing in lads who respected him rather than viewing him as a youngster, he would have grown in confidence and done well. His coaching skills and tactics were always very good, but he wasn't given long enough. Steve Simms arrived as football director during Steve's spell in charge and they never saw eye-to-eye. Steve Mac was shown the door just a year after he got the job.

All this chopping and changing does have an effect on players because, naturally, everyone is worried about where they will stand with the new boss. You generally see players improving their performances when a caretaker coach or a new head coach takes over and that doesn't sit well with me. If I was a coach, I'd look at those lads and wonder if they'd perform like that if my job was under threat or things were going badly. It's alright for players to improve when they're worried about their own positions, but would they do the same for a coach if he was in trouble? In my opinion, players should perform to their best whatever the situation. I've always done that because I think it's only fair.

After Steve, came Karl Harrison and he definitely goes

down as the best club coach I've had. Karl had enormously high standards during his playing days and on the coaching staff at Bradford. He brought those standards to Salford and expected the players to share them. And boy did he have a temper. He used to bring an old fighting sword into video sessions and would threaten you with it if you started messing about. Gareth Haggerty was doing something once that annoyed Karl. Next thing, Karl is whacking the sword down hard on the desk next to Gareth's hand - that certainly got his attention I can tell you. The edges of the sword were blunt, but that didn't mean you weren't scared of it when Karl started wielding it around.

Another time I left my phone on by mistake. I was so paranoid about doing that accidentally that I'd be forever checking the thing and, as bad luck would have it, I knocked it on by accident this particular day. Anyway, it started ringing and you could literally see the steam coming out of Karl's ears. He picked up the TV remote and went to throw it at me. I'm not sure why, but he pulled back at the last second and fined me £40 instead.

As captain, I also had a few ding-dongs with Karl, but I liked that because it allowed me to say things on behalf of the players and Karl could get things off his chest. They usually went like this. I'd let rip and so would Karl. Then we'd both pretend that Karl had won the argument, even if he hadn't. But that's why we worked really well together and it's good for players to have that fear factor of their coach. None of us were over-scared of Karl because he was a real approachable bloke and a good laugh. But you knew where the boundaries were and if you stepped out of line he'd certainly discipline you.

Whereas John Harvey struggled with his malfunctioning tape machine, Karl swept into the Willows with all the latest computer technology and gadgets. It was the sort of equipment most Super League clubs had been using for five years but it opened our eyes at Salford as to how good things could be. Team video sessions were slick and intense and we were also all given our own individual computer analysis, so Karl was very clued up with getting the best out of us on that front.

He also changed our tactical awareness, took us back to the basics and had us really focussing on defending our line. The other good thing Karl later did, particularly from my point of view, was bringing in Jimmy Lowes as his assistant. While Karl was terrific on the defence, Jimmy added to our tactics in attack; the two of them worked very well together. Jimmy would concentrate on certain areas and allow Karl to stand back and see the bigger picture.

As a hooker, Jimmy was a dream for me and I began to realise what I'd missed out on by snubbing the chance to be his understudy at Bradford. Jimmy showed me bits of his game that he thought he could add to mine, and he used to tell me that I could offer far more than he ever could if I combined both our skills. I knew I could never do that because Jimmy had been such a marvellous player and had such a great career. But it was nice that he was telling me these things and my game really came on under him. He even helped me to develop a kicking game that I'd never had before.

Karl arrived too late in 2002 to save us from relegation but it was no fault of his. He felt as bad as any of us and, let me tell you, relegation is an absolute shocker to stomach. It has a huge effect on your family because suddenly your money drops massively and it means major life-changing decisions have to be made. I was lucky that we had a small mortgage at the time; if I'd had a big one, relegation would have been crucifying. I was also a little naïve the first time we got relegated in that I didn't know exactly what all the terms were when we got back into Super League. But you learn from your mistakes and the next time we got relegated I made sure I knew what wages I'd be on once we got promoted.

It's not just the practical problems that get to you after relegation, there's also the mental side of coping with playing in a lower division. I don't mean to be disrespectful to any club in the National League, as it was known then, but there's not the same buzz as there is in going to places like Wigan, St Helens and Leeds. The whole atmosphere is different and the pressure is different.

Because we'd kept a full-time squad, we were expected to win every week and we were indeed demolishing most sides. But that means you start to lose the fear factor. The games are okay, you automatically just switch on. But you can lose your bite in the build-up and it's harder to get yourself up for matches. It really tests your professionalism and that's where Karl was great because he could spot if we weren't quite at the races in training. If he thought we weren't putting in the work, he'd come down very hard by making training exceedingly tough and by putting pressure on us at the right times.

During 2003, we won the National League Cup, beating Leigh 36-19 in extra-time. We'd been leading for much of the 80 minutes but then Leigh took the lead and we needed a last-minute penalty from John Wilshere to level the scores. After that, we then went on to win quite comfortably. We also won the Cup again in 2008, beating Doncaster 60-0 and I admit that I loved the experience both times. I've always tried to treat every game in the same professional manner and not put too much importance on Cup games, just because they are do or die. I've seen players heap too much pressure on themselves by doing that, but I do remember the enormous feeling of relief and achievement of finally winning something. We never managed to do it often enough at Salford, but those Cup wins did make me look more enviously at the captains of clubs who win a lot. I really envy the likes of Kevin Sinfield and Adrian Morley for their experience of lifting the Challenge Cup and Grand Final trophy.

At the end of the 2003 season we also had the enormous relief of promotion. There had been a lot of pressure on us to go up because our livelihoods were at stake, but suddenly we faced different pressures and the tricky situation of how to deal with a dreadful start in which we lost nine out of our first ten games in 2004. Karl's answer was to train us even harder and it didn't go down well with everyone because some people thought it was our tough training sessions that were having an adverse effect on our performances. But Karl was proved right in the second half of the season, when we won plenty of games and finished ninth in the table.

The following year, 2005, we ended up ninth again and in 2006 got our best ever Super League finish of fifth. It's funny because, apart from David Hodgson on the wing, you can't really say anybody had an individually outstanding season. But as a team we all excelled and proved that Karl's big belief in defence does work. We out-defended teams and ground them down by doing the little things right. In training, all we concentrated on was doing the basics well and working really hard. We had a lot of players who, with no disrespect, were not big names but who could be relied on to do their jobs consistently. Lads like Chris Charles and Simon Baldwin were never going to be headline-grabbers, but they were really solid and that's why we did so well.

Which, of course, is partly why I turned down St George-Illawarra. And it was a success that would soon turn sour for Karl too. In May 2007 Salford decided to give him the push. I vividly recall his leaving speech and the embarrassment I felt. Karl sat on the table in the video room and said his goodbyes to us and it was all quite moving. Karl wasn't crying, he's not that type of bloke, but he was emotional and I just sat there thinking that we'd all let him down. I stood up and told the players that it was us who had got him the sack. But unfortunately when players don't perform it's often the coaches who cop the blame.

I'm still friends with Karl and his family and it's really good to see him back in coaching, where he belongs. He was out of the circle for quite a while and once you are out of it, it's very hard to get back in, but Karl deserves another chance and I hope he does well at Halifax.

We all thought that Jimmy would be appointed caretaker coach when Karl left; why wouldn't he, with all his expertise and experience? But Steve Simms, who acted as caretaker after both John Harvey and Steve McCormack left, decided he'd take over again. Why, I'm not quite sure, because he is definitely the worst coach I've ever been under. But anyway he was in charge and started degrading Jimmy by telling him, in front of all the players, that he had to put out cones and menial stuff like that. The players respected Jimmy but many didn't respect Steve and he copped a lot of criticism behind his back as a result of that. Jimmy applied for the head coach's job but we knew he wouldn't get it. If Simms didn't trust him to be caretaker then he was never going to appoint him as head coach. It was sad to see Jimmy leave but we were all glad when he got a job at Warrington.

A month later we were told that Shaun McRae was our new coach. At the time, I didn't know him personally, only by reputation for what he'd done at St Helens, Gateshead and Hull. But Shaun has since become a good mate of mine. It's a great shame that the lack of proper resources at Salford stopped him being the coach we all expected him to be.

Shaun was another Aussie who didn't like the rain. He would often conduct sessions from behind glass in the offices at the training ground, as he sheltered from the downpours. All we'd see was him tapping his watch, indicating that we'd got to carry on for a while yet.

After Karl's high-tech review sessions we were suddenly back to the whiteboard and talking from Shaun - and boy can Shaun talk. He could send a glass eye to sleep. It didn't take long for the lads to realise that nobody should ask any questions otherwise we'd be stuck there for hours. I don't know if Shaun ever cottoned on as to why we all just sat there like nodding dogs, keeping schtum.

Shaun had superb knowledge, though, of virtually any player you could mention. Whoever we were due to meet he could tell you exactly how they played, whether they were left or right-footed, whether they carried the ball with one or two hands and so on and so forth. Endless information.

Shaun is one of life's lovely guys. He's very laid back but great at man-management and getting players to play for him. He was also brilliant in rallying round after Salford got rid of me. But where he fell down badly was in his absolute dislike of disciplining players. I don't think a coach can be like that. He preferred it for Steve Simms to hand out the rollickings, but that meant there was no fear factor like we'd had with Karl. If he ever did try to bollock you he'd do it as a joke, so it never felt like you were being told off. And because so few players seemed to respect Simms, that didn't work either; players would just roll their eyes and say he should fuck off back to Australia.

Simms is an expert at manipulating situations to his own advantage and, in my opinion, Shaun went wrong by not being strong enough with him from the start. Simms would sign players and not even consult Shaun - how bad is that for a head coach? Can you imagine somebody turning up for training at Wigan or South Sydney Rabbitohs and telling Michael Maguire that he's his new player? It wouldn't happen and it shouldn't happen but Shaun allowed it to go on.

Shaun also wasn't helped by lack of finances and I know the squad came nowhere near the salary cap. But where I thought criticism of Shaun was unfair was over the work he did for Sky. If we had been winning regularly, he wouldn't have copped any flak, but because we were losing people claimed he should be concentrating on us instead. I saw it as a positive; Shaun helped to raise the club's profile.

Our next coach I definitely do not rate, as you have no doubt guessed. But Steve Simms has had his hands on the tiller so many times at Salford that I've got to mention him. Four times he took over as caretaker while I was at the club, including when I was assistant, and I still don't think he can coach for toffee. I wouldn't wipe my arse on his gameplans.

Sometimes, you might just as well have told the players to go out and do whatever they wanted. His whiny voice drove me nuts and most players aren't stupid, they quickly begin to see through people. Whenever Simms took over as caretaker coach he'd become good cop, yet whenever he had his football director's hat on he'd be the bad cop. No player responds to someone who changes as quickly as that and it's also very difficult to trust someone if you can't quite believe they are for real.

Matt Parish took over a few months after I left and he only lasted a few matches before he packed his bags and returned to Australia. I'm not sure of exactly went on, but all I will say is that I'm in no way surprised by rumours of clashes between him and Steve Simms. That's five coaches, including me, that Simms has now outstayed at the club and surely there have got to be questions asked about what is going on there. Simms seems untouchable and I don't think that's right if Salford want to progress.

Karl Harrison

● From a football point of view Malcolm was a coach's dream. He was like a sponge who just wanted to soak up more and more information all the time.

When I arrived at Salford I decided to change quite a lot at the club and some players who had been there all their career might have found those changes hard to accept. Not Malcolm. He was into me all the time for extra info and he just craved any chance he could get to improve his game. I did a lot of video and field work with Malcolm and, without sounding big-headed, his game really came on as a result.

Malcolm is the sort of player that coaches love because he is a winner and will do anything to come out on top. He always set very high standards on the training field and every single session he would want to be the fastest, fittest, toughest and the best player he could possibly be. It's great to have somebody like that who is setting the bar very high for his team-mates, and also bringing those team-mates into line if he doesn't think they are up to scratch.

Malcolm wouldn't shirk away from telling anybody off if he felt they needed it, but he did it in a clever way and he always had enormous respect in the camp. Not only did the other players respect him, they also liked him and that shows the character of the man because he's very single-minded and can be a little bit selfish. But everyone knew he was like that because he always wanted what was best for the team. Malcolm was the ultimate team player and would do anything for his side. He completely bought into the ethos and loyalty to his team-mates and the environment was extremely important to him.

I coached England for a couple of years at the same time as I was at Salford and Malcolm really deserved his call-up. I was convinced he was ready for the next stage, too: the Great Britain squad. I was part of the Great Britain selection committee at the time and pushed for him to be involved. But Malcolm was very unfortunate because there were a lot of quality hookers around like Keiron Cunningham, Jimmy Lowes, Terry Newton and Matt Diskin. Also, there was a tendency to only play one hooker in a game.

I guess Malcolm is best known for his incredible tackling stats, but that's probably the media's fault for mentioning it so often. I would argue that another part of Malcolm's game was even better and that was his distribution of the ball. The accuracy of his passes and the distances he got with them were tremendous and I doubt I've seen anyone better at that aspect of the game.

The other trait that made Malcolm a cut above was his phenomenal toughness. At times he had no right to be on the field his body was that broken, but he would never let anyone down. Even I was staggered when Malcolm insisted on playing just days after an appendix operation. I am all for player welfare and was concerned when he said he wanted to play, so I made him face a series of physical and mental tests before I'd agree. He passed every one. I'm not sure how, having just had the surgery he'd had. And not only did he play, he got the man of the match award as well.

Being the single-minded characters we are, it was always inevitable that Malcolm and me would have words at times, just like every coach does with his senior players. But if ever we had a disagreement I would always do it in private. We'd both air our views and then agree that I was right after all.

Players always knew I had a line they couldn't cross and anybody who went near it would get a warning. Anybody who stepped on it would be hit with the stick. Anybody who crossed it would find very big issues with me. But Malcolm never crossed it - he might have stepped on it once or twice but that was it.

As for his drinking, which he has openly admitted could be a problem for him at times, I can honestly say that I never had an issue with him over it. He may well have been hungover at times in training, for all I knew, but Malcolm would never show it because he would never admit to any kind of weakness. Actually, now I think about it, I did have one issue with Malcolm's drinking. Three pints of lager is all it takes to get him drunk.

Playing for England 'A" was an honour -
but it wasn't like playing for Great Britain

17

*

Great Britain Cock-Up

One of my biggest regrets is never getting to pull on a Great Britain shirt. But boy did I come close - by about a week, in fact. I was that close to achieving my dream and cocked it up because, once again, I couldn't control my fists.

I was never sent off in my entire career and until then had never been banned but, as fate would have it, I chose the worst possible moment to break that proud duck. Salford were playing Wakefield at the back end of the 2001 season, when our opponents were scrapping for their Super League survival, which they managed after winning 24-20. A fight broke out which drew in several players - including me.

Referee Russell Smith sent off three Salford players, Bobbie Goulding, Graham Holroyd and Stuart Littler, along with Wakefield centre Justin Brooker. I was sinbinned in the game, along with Wakefield's Martin Pearson. I thought that was the end of the matter, but a couple of days later I was cited and, as a result, copped a £500 fine and three-match suspension. It didn't bother me too much because I was caught fair and square on the video throwing punches. I've always been man enough to take the punishment if it's due.

The ban didn't enter my head when Great Britain team manager Phil Clarke phoned me a short while later and said I was being called up for the first Ashes series since 1994, adding that I had a good chance of playing because Keiron Cunningham and Terry Newton were injured. He told me to report for training the following Monday and I came off the phone feeling on top of the world. Playing for Great Britain. How good did that feel?

I was walking on air for the next couple of days as I day-dreamed about making my GB debut and when Phil phoned me up again I presumed he was just calling to finalise the arrangements. How wrong I was. From being as proud and excited as it was possible to be, I slumped to the very depths of disappointment when Phil told me that I wasn't allowed to play because of the suspension.

I had no idea the suspension applied to internationals. To describe it as a gut-wrencher would be the understatement of the decade. I was so gutted I couldn't even bring myself to watch much of that series, because I knew I might never get another chance to push myself into the squad. When you're competing against the likes of Keiron and Terry it's always going to be difficult; you've got to sieze any glimmer of a chance you get. Leeds Rhinos' Kevin Sinfield played hooker instead and that made me feel even worse because number nine isn't even his recognised position.

My disappointment wasn't just limited to missing out on the GB shirt, because the ban also hit me heavily in the pocket. My Salford contract, at the time, included a £12,000 bonus if I made my full Great Britain debut, so my first ever suspension ended up costing me a £500 fine, a £12,000 bonus and, most importantly of all, the chance to represent my country. I couldn't believe it. On top of all that, I still had to serve a three-match suspension at the start of the following season, so it was a double whammy. I missed out on three possible internationals and three Salford games as well. It was a joke, but one that was on me.

I did make two England appearances in 2005, against France and New Zealand, and although I was extremely proud, I have to admit that they didn't feel like the real thing. England was the 'B' team to the Great Britain side at the time, and although we got caps and wore the England shirt, I didn't class them as full internationals. Despite that, you couldn't wipe the smile off my face when I pulled on those England jerseys and I loved the whole experience. Karl Harrison, my Salford coach back then, was in charge and that helped in a way, because I knew what to expect from him and what he demanded from his players. But, also, I would have quite liked to have been under a different coach because then I might have learned something new.

I had discovered what that was like when I made my debut under Ian Millward for Lancashire in the 2002 War of the Roses match against Yorkshire at Headingley. Tactically, Ian was very good but he was also a great man-manager and I felt my game came on a lot from the whole experience.

That Lancashire side was star-studded with the likes of Kris Radlinski, Terry Newton, Barrie McDermott, Terry O'Connor, Andy Farrell... and I admit I was a little in awe of them when I first joined up with the squad. But they were all welcoming and it didn't take me long to feel part of the set-up, especially seeing as Ian had a policy of taking us out drinking so we could gel as a team. I like that sort of team-bonding!

I was named on the bench and Ian later told me he had only planned to bring me on for 20 minutes, but he was so impressed he left me on longer. Hearing that filled me with even more pride and boosted my confidence. From then on I vowed that I wanted more representative rugby and at a higher level too.

The following year, the War of the Roses fixtures came to and end and that was a real shame. When you've got the best 34 players in the country competing against each other you're bound to see an improvement in standards, as each player vies to be the best. It was a no-brainer for me, because I had seen at first hand experience how much it helped my own game and boosted my own determination to succeed. Australia have the State of Origin series and that wasn't a great success when it first started. Yet it has built into a tremendous rivalry and spectacle and one that gives Aussie players a perfect preparation for Test rugby. I really think we should have persevered with the War of the Roses; we might have helped our international hopes into the bargain.

As well as my close brush with Great Britain, I also came close to two other tastes of international competition and once again ended up having my fingers burned.

The disappointment came when Ireland approached me about the possibility of being part of their 2008 World Cup squad. My nan on my mum's side was Irish and there is quite a lot of Irish background in my family, so the eligibity issue wasn't in question. Nor was the fact that I'd already played for England because there had been a long enough gap since I had done so.

My Salford mates Karl Fitzpatrick, who had alerted Ireland to my eligibility, and Stuart Littler were both in the squad and I looked forward to being involved. To qualify for the trip to Australia and New Zealand, I had to have played for Ireland in 2007, so I met up with the relevant people and it was agreed that I would make my Ireland debut.

But those plans were ruined when I injured my shoulder and needed reconstruction surgery at the end of the season.

That was that. Ireland went off to the World Cup without me and did really well with performances that made the whole country proud. I watched them on TV at home knowing I could have been part of it, but I'd realised by that stage that there's no point in worrying about what might have been.

I didn't have that mature attitude, however, ten years earlier when I suffered a real kick in the teeth after being told that I was to play in the 1997 World Club Challenge down under. The competition involved 22 teams from Australia and England, as well as Paris St Germain, and to say I was excited beyond belief is an understatement. At the age of 18, it was a dream to think that I could play in Australia and, hopefully, see some of the game's greatest players in action at close quarters.

I'd had to get a passport and had already sorted out exactly what I would be packing for the trip when Andy Gregory called me in and said he was dropping me from the squad. I couldn't believe it and, to this day, still have a beef with Greg about the way he treated me. It's the only time he ever let me down and I thought his reason for leaving me out was pretty shoddy. A few days earlier he'd signed a winger called Richard Smith on loan and he took my place.

That was Greg's perogative as coach, I suppose, but I was absolutely gutted and felt he'd let me down. The team were hammered 50-8 by Adelaide Rams and 44-8 by North Queensland Cowboys in Townsville, but it didn't make me feel any better knowing I hadn't been part of a tournament that turned out to be an embarrassment for the British clubs. Then, to make matters worse, Greg let Richard Smith go a week after they got back from Australia. Losing out to a player who would play a big role in Salford's history would have been hard to stomach, but to lose out to a lad who was only there a few weeks felt so much worse.

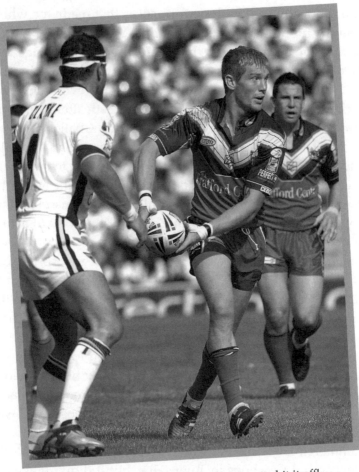

Me and the lurking Jon Clarke never quite hit it off!

18

*

Fights, Fists and F**k - Ups!

Even though the game is so brutal and everyone plays it hard, there are very few on-going feuds between players. I've never really had a problem with anyone, with the exception of Jon Clarke.

For some reason, we never hit it off in the early days when Jon was at Wigan, before he moved to London Broncos and then Warrington, where he had such a great career that is still going on at Widnes. Maybe we were too similar, but every time we played each other we clashed and we would be head-butting each other in the scrums and bad-mouthing each other, trying to wind one another up.

One night, the Salford team was on its way back from a game in London and Stuart Littler suggested we stop for a few drinks in Leigh, so we got the bus driver to drop us off. The ale had been flowing on the coach and we loaded up our bags with cans (I've never been one to turn down a freebie!) and headed into a boozer that seemed pretty lively. Jon was in there with a few of his mates and we didn't really take each other on until me and Stu left and Jon came over and started saying he wanted to sort things out. I told him it should stay on the field but Jon was saying he was a street fighter so, without warning, I dropped my bag and banged him one when he wasn't ready. He went down and we started scrapping on the ground and it got pretty intense as we were both pretty decent fighters. It would have probably all been sorted out with only a few cuts and bruises if I hadn't been wearing flip-flops - what stupid sod gets into a street brawl in flip-flops? I didn't have any grip at all, but because we were rolling about on the ground, throwing punches at each other, I had to try and get some purchase by digging my toes into the ground. At the time, because of the adrenalin, I didn't notice the pain, but when we eventually finishing fighting I looked at my feet and they were ripped to shreds. Jon went off with a cut under his eye, while I pretended I was fine. Really, I was in sheer agony.

John Harvey was the Salford coach at the time and it didn't take him long to smell a rat when I turned up in bare feet, telling him I couldn't train. I couldn't even put on my socks or trainers, and could only move by hobbling badly. John wanted to know what had happened, so I told him a story I'd practised about a taxi running over my feet. Even as I was saying it I could tell John didn't believe a word - not surprising, really - but he asked me again if it was genuine and I put on my best choirboy's face and said: 'Yes John, that's definitely what happened.' He gave a wry smile and went off to find Stuart Littler, who he knew I'd got off the coach with.

A few minutes later Stu comes up to me and says he told John that I was getting out of a taxi when I got caught in the door and the taxi drove off, dragging me along the road. As my face fell, Stu said: 'But that's what we agreed to say!' I knew the game was up, so I went and told John the truth and, to be fair to him, he was alright about it and said we'd try and keep it quiet. I couldn't train all week but I managed to get the last session in and got picked for that weekend's game. Boy, did my feet hurt during that match.

At the time it didn't seem great but, funnily enough, that fight was the best thing for me and Jon because later we met again and had a good old laugh about it. Maybe we just needed to let off steam. Ever since, we've been as right as rain. We still got a few digs in, of course, in the scrums; that's what you did in the early days. The scrums have cleaned up massively now because the game is so fast, but back then all sorts went on... nipping, kicking, standing on feet and head-butting.

I was given my scrum apprenticeship by two of the hardest men in the game, props Andy Platt and Cliff Eccles. They showed me how to get away with punching without the ref spotting. They would hold me up and I'd release both arms so I could get a few good hits in on their front row. If the ref did happen to spot it, you'd leave your arm locked around the prop nearest the ref and release the other one. The back-rowers were also pretty handy at punching in the scrum and I've copped a fair few clean shots in my time. Nowadays the scrums are so clean that you go in there for a rest, but in the old days a rest was the last thing you got. They could end up as all-out fighting sessions.

On the subject of refs and officials, I'd like to mention Ian Blease, one of the nicest and most honest blokes I had the pleasure of playing with. That may sound a little weird given that many fans will remember Ian for infamously getting banned for life for assaulting a touch judge during a reserve game against Bradford in 1997. Ian later got it reduced to ten months on appeal, a decision I was pleased about because I saw what happened and it didn't totally surprise me that Ian lost his cool. Some of the decisions that were being made in the game were absolutely atrocious and everybody was getting frustrated. So when a touch judge gave yet another dodgy decision, Ian just lost it and gave him a back hander across his face. To say we were all gobsmacked was an understatement because everybody knows you can't touch an official, and rightly so. We could all see straight away by the look on Ian's face that he knew he was in major trouble and we all felt sorry for him because we knew how much he'd been getting wound up.

Although Ian will be remembered by a lot of people just for that reason, I prefer to remember him as the bloke who went out of his way to help kids coming through like me. He would often take me to one side, as well as any other young player who had broken into the first team squad, and give you loads of advice and help on what you should or shouldn't be doing. He was one of the most encouraging team-mates I've ever had and was a role model to us all because he was such a clean-living bloke. He'd have a drink, of course, but Ian always knew when to stop. It's just a real shame that his career at Salford ended in the way it did.

Ian's rare loss of control cost him a lot, whereas my frequent fights have mostly been off the field and not as damaging. Career-wise that is, because a fair few of my fights have definitely been physically damaging.

One night me, my brother Melvin and the Salford conditioner Mick Sutherland were out drinking in Tyldesley when Mick got into a scuffle with a bloke outside a pub. Me and Melvin went outside to help him but the other bloke ran back into the pub and then reappeared with a huge group of mean-looking fellas. Just by looking at them we knew we had bitten off more than we could chew and they quickly got me and Melvin down on the ground and started kicking us in the ribs and back and stamping on our heads. We could see each other as we lay on the ground and in our eyes we both knew that we feared we were goners, the beating we were getting was that bad. If it hadn't been for the bouncers pulling them off us, I really don't know if we'd have come out of that kicking in one piece.

Now, I've mentioned before that Melvin is a bit of a head-the-ball and if ever there was an example that backs up that claim it's this one. Most blokes in their right mind would have been relieved that the bouncers had come to the rescue and left it at that. Not our Melvin! A van had arrived for the other blokes and as they're getting in Melvin rushes over to them and starts throwing punches. I couldn't leave him to get battered again on his own, so without thinking (that's the story of my life!) I went to join him - and also got leathered. For the second time. And still our Melvin doesn't see any sense because as the van pulls away down the street Melvin starts running after it, yelling for them to stop and fight. I think that even the blokes had realised by this point that Melvin wasn't totally sane and drove off, to my relief, I have to admit. Two batterings in one night is more than enough for me.

An ambulance had been called and Mick, who hadn't come to our aid even though he started all the trouble, was on the verge of tears because his ear had got cut in the original scuffle. The ambulance worker took one look at it and told him he was fine and then turned to me and Melvin and told us to get into the ambulance because we needed hospital treatment. I had a massive wound on my head that wouldn't stop bleeding. I needed 36 stitches in that and various other cuts, while Melvin needed a dozen or so stitches in his head too.

As is always the case with me, the trouble doesn't stop when the fighting stops because I always have to go into training the day after and try to avoid facing the music. I put on a baseball cap for probably the first time in my life and that immediately set the alarm bells ringing for coach Steve McCormack, who told me to take it off. I looked like something off Michael Jackson's *Thriller* video, but Steve just shook his head and said he'd cover for me. That was good of him and a sign of a strong players' coach.

Straight after training I told Melvin I'd got off lightly and then we set about trying to find out who the blokes were who'd given us such a hiding. We never did discover their names, but I still remember what they look like. All I'll say is I'm someone who holds a grudge with a long memory. I'm still keeping my eyes open for a bloke I lent £20 to, and didn't get it back, when I was 18. I've no problems lending people money, but they always have to repay it and, even if I'm pissed, there's no chance of me forgetting because I text Sonia straight away and tell her who's borrowed it.

Another time one of my Salford pals got me into trouble - and then failed to help me out - was on a night out in Wigan, with Melvin and Neil Baines. We were eating pizzas outside a takeaway in King Street when Neil, who can put away a fair few in one go, was accused by this girl of calling her a slag. Anyway, she was livid and really surprised Neil by laying into him big time, giving him a real belting. Me and Melvin dragged her off but a group of lads thought we were having a go at her, which we weren't, so they piled in and started fighting us! I tell you, I might start having to decide who's safe to go out with in future. Neil was conspicuous by his absence as the fists flew, which pissed me off. But not nearly as much as the broken hand I ended up with and the brush with the cops later that night.

When me and Melvin eventually got back to his house he realised he'd forgotten his keys, so he climbed through a window and was nicked by passing coppers who thought he was a burglar. The following day I phoned Karl Harrison, the coach, to mention that I'd been in a bit of bother, but didn't mention the broken hand as he'd have lost his rag big time if he'd known. I had pain-killing injections without Karl knowing and managed to train and play the next game. I thought I'd got away with it until Steve Simms hauled me up. He'd been playing golf with Wigan's Mike Forshaw who told him everything. I was furious and the next time I saw Mike I told him, in no uncertain terms, that I wasn't happy at being grassed up, but he claimed he thought Steve knew anyway. It still wasn't on though. I was reminded of that incident a few years later when I heard that Neil Baines had told people that me and Melvin beat him up that night. I've no idea why he should say that, unless he was embarrassed about being beaten up by a girl, but I was filthy about it. He'd left Salford by that time, so I never did have it out with him. But I've certainly not forgotten, Neil.

Most of my team-mates have always been as good as gold when it comes to helping each other and Karl Fitzpatrick and Stuart Littler are two of the best. I was in a club once when the bouncers threw me down the steps for falling asleep, which was like a red rag to a bull. I started fighting all of them. Fitzy and Stu immediately helped me out and I ended up needing six stitches in my head and Fitzy had a deep gash under his eye, which he's still got the scar from to this day. The next day at training, Karl Harrison spotted Fitzy's gash and demanded to know how he got it. So I owned up, told him it was my fault, and Karl said that was the end of the matter. It wasn't for me, though. Someone sent Steve Simms an email saying they'd seen me fighting and I ended up copping a fine.

That's the trouble when you're fairly well known. You get recognised easily and sometimes that can mean bother from blokes who fancy proving how tough they are. One night, me and Tony Stewart, David Hodgson and Luke Robinson were out in Bolton when a complete stranger started threatening us for no reason. Tony can throw a mean punch if he has to, but he's fairly placid so he just let this bloke carry on verbally abusing him. Realising he's not getting anywhere with Tony, the bloke then turns his abuse on me and you know what's coming next - I headbutted him and down he went. I know I should have taken Tony's lead and let it wash over me, but I've always had a short fuse. If I feel threatened, I'll fight my corner no matter what the consequences. At least that night I did have the good sense to leave straight after the head-butt and we all grabbed a taxi and left before it got any worse.

The only fight I've ever regretted was in the Walkabout pub in Wigan. Yet again, a total stranger started yelling abuse and trying to goad me. For once, I tried to ignore him and turned away; he was obviously just a nutcase. But he wouldn't shut up and eventually my patience snapped. I swung round and landed a cracking knockout blow. The only trouble was that the bloke now on the deck seeing stars was the wrong man. I knocked out some innocent bloke who just happened to be walking past. I knew I was in big lumber so I legged it out of the pub and phoned Sonia, telling her to come and get me because I was in a bit of bother. Two days later the phone went and it was some bloke who played for Wigan St Judes demanding to know why I had punched his lights out. He was pretty angry and all I could do was grovel and apologise and say I'd hit the wrong man. Eventually he accepted it, which was good of him considering he'd had to go to hospital in an ambulance.

Battering the wrong person though must be a family trait because Melvin also did it when we were both teenagers. We were drinking in Mirage in Standish when we thought we'd spotted a bloke who had just dumped our cousin after treating her pretty badly. Melvin said he wanted to teach him a lesson and belted him, which got the bouncers involved. We both ended up fighting them, even though I'd recently dislocated my shoulder and had my arm tucked inside my shirt as a sling. Afterwards, me and Melvin were chatting and we agreed that we'd taught our cousin's 'ex' a lesson about not messing girls about. But the next day we found out we'd hit the wrong bloke and I discovered that I'd set my shoulder rehab back by several weeks.

You would think that recapping all my fights (and there are far too many to mention them all) would make me see sense and learn how to control my temper. But even when I was on the coaching staff at Salford, I could still find myself in trouble. Me and my brothers Melvin and Marlon went to watch the darts at the *Manchester Evening News* Arena and we were having a good time until Melvin started talking to some bloke. I'd gone to the bar and had the drinks on a tray when this bloke is suddenly in my face saying: 'Who the fucking hell are you?' That's all I needed to react. I dropped the tray of drinks and gave him a pasting, knocking out some of his teeth. I know I should handle these things better but I'd never dream of talking to someone like that.

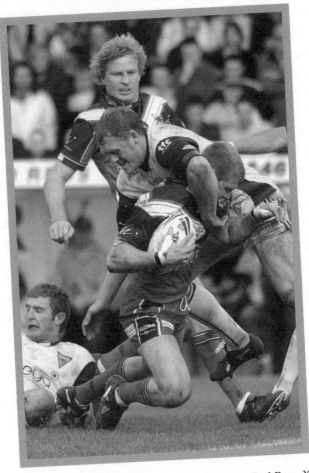

Ouch! Ben Westwood makes my Super League Bad Boys XIII

19

*

My Super League Bad Boys XIII

Given my love of a beer and a fight, I couldn't resist the temptation to draw up a dream team of similar nutcases - players who have just been downright stupid on or off the field; players who love a drink or 20; the players who can go crackers for no apparent reason. There are also a fair few in this team who have spent time at Her Majesty's pleasure. Draw your own conclusions about the part beer has played.

FULL BACK - BEN COCKAYNE
Ben can be a bit handy with his fists, on the field and off it, as his time behind bars proved. I don't know him personally, although I really rate him as a player.

WINGERS - JOEL MONAGHAN and GARETH RAYNOR
Well come on, isn't it obvious why Joel is selected? It would have been woof justice if he hadn't been, after his infamous filmed 'romp' with a dog while at Canberra.

Gareth got banged up for selling fake printer ink and then got himself sacked by Bradford after they threw him a lifeline. There's definitely something self-destructive there.

CENTRES - STUART LITTLER and MARTIN GLEESON

Stu, my former Salford mate, is a real contradiction. He's an educated lad and usually the most level-headed of blokes, but when he has a drink he becomes as daft as a brush. I also quickly learnt that Stu likes to cause a fight and then, when it all kicks off, he's nowhere to be seen! Very gobby and antagonistic on the pitch too. I was always glad he was a team-mate and not an opponent.

Glees walks into this team thanks to his involvement in the St Helens betting scandal, frequent booze-related trouble and the Hull cover-up controversy. He also used to wind his clubs up with his inability to turn up for training on time.

STAND OFF - SEAN LONG

Gets in with Glees for his ridiculous naiveté in putting on a bet against his own team in his own name. I mean, how daft can you get? Then there are the many drinking escapades...

SCRUM HALF - LEE BRIERS

Lee only just hangs on to his place because he's calmed down a lot under the influence of Tony Smith at Warrington. But stories of his partying before Tony arrived were legendary, so I reckon he still deserves his spot.

PROPS - RYAN BAILEY and DANNY SCULTHORPE

Ryan has to be one of the most unpopular players in Super League. He makes a lot of high tackles and I don't know whether that's down to poor technique, fatigue, downright clumsiness or maliciousness. He regularly winds opponents up. Maybe he thinks he has to live up to some sort of hard man image, but that's not how hard men play. Bailey puts his team under pressure which is stupidity, not toughness.

To be fair, Danny only just made the team because, bizarrely, I was struggling to think of another out-and-out prop headcase, which is odd in itself. But Danny certainly liked to party in his day and he gets in for that reason.

HOOKER - TERRY NEWTON

Terry was like me in that he always got giddy with a drink in him and sometimes didn't know when to stop - drinking or fighting. As a player, he could also be quite handy. Remember that infamous incident when he broke Sean Long's cheekbone? And they were supposed to be mates!

SECOND ROW - GARETH HOCK and BEN WESTWOOD

Gareth is my captain, he's that daft. Got a two-year ban for taking cocaine and then ends his comeback early by getting a five-match ban for eye gouging and punching, ruining his hopes of an England call-up. Has he no sense? It seems not, because he also copped a five-game ban for manhandling a referee in 2008.

Benny is the man who Hock punched and it's a wonder he didn't flatten him back. He is a real tough bloke on the field, but he gets in my team because he's also very loose off the field when he has a few drinks. Benny is a big party animal who, like Briers, has calmed the excesses since Tony Smith took control.

LOOSE FORWARD - DANNY TICKLE

Danny is a great player but another who gets in because of his love of a good party. He can get very giddy when he's under the influence.

At Salford, I didn't need much of an excuse to party

20

✻

Losing the Captaincy

I can look back now and realise how mad all the drugs were but, at the time, you are so caught up in it all that you think it's almost normal. Even to the point where players would often have 'sleeper parties', where half the people would end up in a right old mess on a combination of alcohol and sleeping tablets.

I had one at my house at the end of 2009 as a leaving party for Craig Stapleton, one of our Aussie players. We had become pretty good mates, most of the lads turned up and the sleepers started getting handed out. I didn't take any because I was hosting the party and sleepers can either send me really tired or daft. Either way, it wouldn't have looked good if the party host was out if it.

Several of my team-mates, however, were wandering about like zombies as the night wore on and Sonia gradually had enough, because she was heavily pregnant at the time, and took herself off to bed. She was really tired and, despite the noise, fell asleep until she became aware of somebody trying to get into bed with her, and it certainly wasn't me. The sight of big daft Ray Cashmere trying to get into bed with you would scare anybody, especially when you are nearly about to give birth, but Sonia was furious and she gave him a right earful before sending him packing. Ray came back downstairs and I didn't have a clue about what had happened until much later when I eventually went to bed and Sonia, who was still seething, told me. I don't think I helped the situation by laughing, but when you are totally pissed things like that do seem amusing.

The other memorable moment from Ray that night was the sight of him trying to attack my Staffordshire bull terrier, Taz. As you can imagine, Taz wasn't too thrilled at the idea of this huge clumsy bloke trying to rugby-tackle him, so he kept running away, which only spurred Ray on more. The next day, I naturally brought up both incidents and Ray couldn't remember a thing. He later did a bit of grovelling to Sonia, but he decided to leave Taz alone. Apologising to one victim was enough.

As the party was at my house, I was more restrained than I often am - like for, instance, the time I went to the Salford Christmas party at a boozer in Eccles and tackled the huge Christmas tree. The lads dared me to do it and if there's one thing I can't resist, it's a dare. But I decided to go one better and stripped off to my underpants before charging full pelt and toppling the thing over. The pub was absolutely packed and, by this stage there was tinsel and baubles all over the place, but that didn't stop the rest of the team from piling in and trying to rip off my underpants. Having a fight in the middle of all those needles, while trying to hold on to your undies, isn't the most respectable way to pass the festive season, but the landlord was fine about it all. He knew me from previous escapades, so he wasn't totally surprised.

The one person who was surprised by my antics at that

party, though, was our forward, Mark Edmondson. He was on the telephone to his missus when I grabbed his mobile and plonked it in a pint of beer, knackering it completely. He'd only joined us that year and I don't think he knew how to take me. He just looked at me and didn't say a thing. We had a laugh about it much later but he never did ask me to buy him a new one - he probably knew he had two chances of that happening. Fat chance and no chance.

The more I got to know Mark, the more I realised I didn't know him at all. In fact, it wouldn't be too far from the point to call him a bit of a weirdo, even though he was a lovely lad. How else can you explain his behaviour during one of our pre-season training trips to Jacksonville, Florida?

A few of us got back late to the hotel from a night out, and as we were walking through the foyer we spotted Mark in one of the glass elevators, covered in a blanket. As he seemed to be heading down to reception, we thought we'd wait and ask him what he was doing. We quickly realised that Mark was only wearing swimming trunks, apart from the blanket he was clutching. He didn't appear to be drunk and there weren't any other lads hanging about, so it didn't appear to be some sort of dare he was carrying out.

'What are you up to?' we asked. Sober as a judge, Mark replied 'I'm a mermaid' and walked across to the fountain in the foyer. We were almost hysterical with laughter as we watched him drop his blanket, climb into the water and start thrashing about. But there's only so long you can watch a grown man pretending to be a mermaid in six inches of water, so we left him to it and went off to bed. To this day, he still hasn't told us what he was playing at.

Jacksonville was later to be the scene of one of the lowest points in my career - the loss of the Salford captaincy - but before then, those pre-season trips were absolutely fantastic. We would train hard in that gorgeous weather but under

Karl Harrison we would also be allowed to party hard, as long as we were all bang on the money in training the next day. And because Karl treated us like that, we were always good as gold and worked until we were fit to drop. We also revelled in Karl's emphasis on ball handling skills, as well as the grind of the usual pre-season slog.

On one of the trips under Karl all the lads split into two groups; one lot sightseeing and the usual suspects having a drinking session in one of the hotel bedrooms (no prizes for guessing which group I was in). We started a game where you had to sit with a cardboard beer box on your head and had to pay a fine if you took it off or it fell off. We had Andrew, the middle-aged disabled son of vice-chairman Howard Clague, with us and he always loved the craic of being with the lads, even though there was little he could actually do because of his disabilities. He is in a wheelchair, can only speak with the aid of a machine and drink through a straw, but we treated him as one of the lads and I think he really appreciated how we included him in our fun. Andrew was also sitting there with a box on his head and having a great time when I got a message that Karl, Jimmy Lowes and Howard needed to see me for a meeting about team plans. But no way was I going to pay a fine for taking the box off. So I strolled into the meeting with it still on my head, as if it was the most normal thing in the world. I told Karl what it was about and he was cool, but the other lads clearly didn't trust me. Throughout the meeting, they kept wandering past checking that I'd still got it on my head. Let me tell you, when it comes to money there's no way I'll give anything up easily. Gareth Haggerty eventually lost and, as his fine, had to buy a round of drinks and down a huge quantity of beer in one go.

But when Shaun McRae arrived at Salford, it changed for the worse. Shaun tried to ban drinking on the trip. Can you imagine a bunch of grown blokes not being allowed to drink on a long trip like that? It was never going to happen, but it wasn't resolved properly and the players just ended up in revolt, going behind Shaun's back. I hadn't thought it was fair that the players were being stopped from drinking if the coaches were allowed booze, so as captain I protested and the coaches agreed that they would also stick to Shaun's ban. Yeah, right! Us players would have a couple of quiet drinks and one night we bumped into some of the coaches, who had also gone for a crafty few pints in a bar. Alan Hunte was one and he even had the nerve to grass us up to Scott Naylor the next day (he's clearly not the brightest spark because, naturally, I then grassed him in too). It was all a mess but Shaun would simply try and pretend that he didn't know anybody was drinking.

Me and Robbie Paul did give it away big style on one trip though, when Shaun caught us absolutely drunk out of our heads at 11 o'clock one morning (it was a day off). We'd been on the Jack Daniels from the previous evening and hadn't got a clue what time it was when we decided it would be a good idea to do some shadow boxing. Robbie only had his underpants on and I was in my shorts when we went out of Robbie's room. The hotel was designed with the rooms on four sides and a walkway overlooking the central square. Oblivious to anything else, including the families and kids milling about, we started boxing and practising our tackling technique. We didn't realise that Shaun had spotted us and his patience finally ran out when me and Robbie devised this game where we would start at opposite corners of the quadrangle and then run full pelt and collide with each other. He bellowed at us to get back to our rooms but, rather than take the bollocking, we decided to get dressed and head off to a nearby mall for more booze and a spot of shopping. By this stage we'd been drinking solid for about

18 hours when Robbie suddenly went back to the hotel to sober up, leaving me with his shopping bags. Without him to chat to and laugh with, I suddenly started to feel tired, so I laid down in the mall entrance and promptly fell asleep (as you do). Apparently, shoppers were stepping over me and I must have looked like some sort of down and out. But I was so zonked that it hardly even registered when, at one point, some of the other lads turned up shopping and were very amused when they spotted me. They man-handled me into a minibus they'd arrived in to sleep it off out of the public eye.

As well as the booze, there were also plenty of women available for any blokes who were interested, including prostitutes who would openly cruise the hotel corridors looking for customers - most blokes wouldn't touch them with a barge pole. But some of the younger lads certainly got up to some action with the opposite sex, including with one unfortunate girl. Why this particular player thought I'd be interested, I have absolutely no idea, but I was woken one night by this lad telling me to come and look at this girl in his bed... and what some of the lads had done to her with a banana. I'll leave the rest to your imagination but I certainly wasn't interested and told the lad to rectify the situation before she woke up as she might not be best pleased. He was really pissed off with me because I wouldn't get out of bed and went away moaning that, as captain, I was letting the team down. But some things just don't come into the job description of captain and seeing a young lass degraded is one of them.

Under Karl, we always used to split into groups and do sketches and skits in front of the rest of the squad towards the end of the trip and it would be fantastic for team bonding. When Shaun took over, we tried to do the same in his first trip but it just didn't work when we were all sober so that little tradition ended pretty quickly. The trip that left a bad taste in my mouth, and caused huge problems at the club, was the one before the 2009 season. Things got pretty wild even on the flight out to America because a few of us decided to celebrate the news that my brother Marlon's missus had just found out she was expecting. Marlon was trying to force his way into the team at that stage and we were all made up for him that life seemed to be pretty good at home as well as at work. But most of us had taken sleeping tablets for the long flight and, when we then started necking the wine as well, we were soon pretty blasted and our behaviour got very rowdy. I know it wasn't correct behaviour for professionals, representing our club, but at the time it just seemed to be a laugh and I wasn't aware of any other passengers complaining.

Nobody from the club said anything to us but our behaviour had clearly been noted and it was later held against me when other things started to go wrong. The other thing that bugs me is that when we arrived at Florida, Steve Simms told me I couldn't drive one of the team vehicles but didn't try to stop me when I insisted, even though he knew I was drunk. I'm not proud of driving in that condition because I knew I could have caused some serious damage, and I clearly wasn't in a fit state because I almost fell asleep at one point and Craig Stapleton had to take over.

During the trip, Shaun approved a rare official day off when we could drink. After a session, me, Marlon, Willie Talau and John Wilshere hailed a taxi to try and find a nightclub we'd been told about. We didn't know what it was called, so I told the taxi driver that it was a new black hip hop dance club and suddenly John started to go berserk, calling me a racist for the way I'd described the club. I couldn't believe my ears because there's no way I'm racist, but he continued with the abuse until I couldn't stand it any more and I told the driver to stop the taxi so me and John could sort things out. I grabbed him and was just warning him that I could have easily belted him there and then when he punched me smack in the face. That was the signal for it all to kick off and I ended up giving him a bit of a beating. It was nothing too major - he went on to the nightclub - but I returned to the hotel to sober up as I knew I'd overstepped the line as captain. Never before had I had a fight with one of my own team-mates; I knew I was in big trouble.

I wanted to be ready for whatever might happen later, but my mood wasn't helped by the abusive texts I kept getting from John. After a while I'd had enough and decided to go looking for him, but thankfully I couldn't find him and once more returned to the hotel and ordered a few more coffees. Marlon and Craig Stapleton, meanwhile, had nipped out to get a McDonalds and they got back just as Phil Leuluai, Willie Talau and John Wilshere did.

For some reason, the three of them jumped Craig, breaking his nose and blackening his eyes. Marlon came running to get me and a few of the other players and we all ran down to find Craig in a right mess. Phil and Willie shot off but John, who was very drunk, started verbally abusing me again, although he was so wasted I could see there was no point even arguing with him. I'd never had trouble from him before, but alcohol can change people, me included.

The hotel called the police and the cops actually told us to go to a local golf course and sort it out between ourselves, but John didn't want to. Steve Simms had apparently been watching everything from a balcony and I discovered the next day that John told Steve I'd kicked him in the face. It certainly wasn't true; if I had you'd have been able to tell just by looking at him.

Anyway, I knew I hadn't acted as a captain should, by fighting a team-mate and I told the players that I was willing to hand in the captaincy. I left the decision up to them but they wouldn't decide and instead left it up to the club. But, whoever made the decision, I knew the armband would be taken off me and quite rightly so. That behaviour should never have happened and I fully accepted the punishment. I was gutted, of course, but I took it on the chin and vowed to make the club realise what they had lost.

The disappointment spurred me on even more and I got the man of the match award in our first game of the new season against Celtic Crusaders. I wasn't bitter because I deserved to be punished, but I wanted to prove a point about how good a captain I'd been and I purposely stopped talking as much and giving my opinions.

Rob Parker was offered the captaincy but he approached me first and asked me what I thought. I told him straight away to take it with both hands and do a good job. Rob is a good mate of mine and I didn't have any problems with him getting the armband because I knew I'd lost it through my own stupidity. But even though Rob didn't do anything wrong, it just didn't work out for him and Shaun asked me to take the captaincy back, telling me he believed I'd learned my lesson. I really didn't know if it was the right thing to do, but Shaun talked me into it and I was just as honoured as I'd always been when I eventually took the role back on.

As well as having the captaincy taken off me, I also faced a legal battle after the club tried to fine me two weeks' wages. In the end, me and Craig Stapleton ended up paying £300 each and John Wilshere was fined too, with Willie Talau and Phil Leuluai also copping an undisclosed fine. It was a messy business all round and the club abandoned the annual Jacksonville trip in 2010. It was probably just as well.

Career-ending injury came in a game with Leeds

21

*

Salford Broke my Heart

The pain was by no means as excruciating as some I've experienced, but I knew I was in trouble when I lost all feeling down the left side of my body. I've had plenty of stingers before and so know what it's like to temporarily lose feeling in your arm, but this was different because this was in my left leg as well.

I hadn't realised what happened at the time, but after watching video replays I discovered that Ali Lauitiiti had shoulder-charged me in the back as I tried to collect a bad pass that had gone behind me. I wasn't expecting the tackle because I didn't have the ball and, because I hadn't tensed in anticipation, it hurt me badly. Little did I know that it was also the injury which would end my Super League playing career and set me on the collision course with Salford that would eventually see me pushed out of a club I had loved for 16 years.

I'm not blaming Lauitiiti at all. These things happen. I was just unlucky in that home game against Leeds Rhinos in

July 2010. The bench could clearly see I was in trouble and the physio rushed on. After a while, as the feeling came back first in my leg and then my arm, I thought I was okay to carry on. Wrong! In the next tackle I went into on my left side, I got knocked clean out and that was that. Forever.

I was left with pins and needles in my hand for about two weeks, but that was a minor problem compared to the news I got from the specialist after I had scans done on my neck. I had two prolapsed discs with one protruding onto a nerve. The stark advice was that I shouldn't play again. It was a bombshell, being told my career was done and dusted and that there was nothing I could do to save it. I couldn't even have one last farewell game to say a fitting goodbye to the fans who had been so loyal to me for so long. That's what was so disappointing; I couldn't bow out on my terms and all because of an injury, when I'd had so few in my career. If I'd got it two years earlier I'd have had no problem coming back at some stage, but happening at the time it did was a real blow. And although it certainly wasn't the most painful injury I'd ever had, the consequences hit me in more long-lasting ways than I could ever have anticipated.

Coming four weeks before the end of the 2010 season, it also gave me the answer to a question I'd been wrestling with for a while - whether to stay on with Salford's coaching staff or take up a probable offer of a two-year deal at Hull. I'd met Hull coach Richard Agar a few times and it looked like they were going to make a firm bid, but I planned to leave the decision until the end of the season so I could give myself every chance to know in my own mind whether I could play on for two more years, or whether it would be wiser to take a full-time off-field role.

The injury made my mind up for me and now I'll never know whether it would have worked out for me at Hull. But at the time I wasn't too gutted. I was happy at the thought of becoming a full-time coach after spending the 2010 season combining being a player with acting as Shaun McRae's assistant. His unpaid assistant, I should point out.

In typical Salford style, I felt I was manipulated a little into accepting the job on an unpaid basis, but I was keen to get my foot on the first rung of the coaching ladder so I hadn't kicked up a fuss. Once again, that loyalty to the club was to come back and haunt me.

Scott Naylor had been Shaun McRae's assistant, after first being appointed by Karl Harrison, and Scott was very good on the coaching side. But he let himself down with his man-management skills and often came into training in bad moods. His grumpiness would affect the players at times. The board had obviously got wind that everything wasn't as it should be and, at the end of 2009, one of the directors phoned and asked me what I thought of Scott.

I will stress here that there was no way I was angling for Scott's job. The idea hadn't even entered my head. At that stage I thought I still had a few years left in me as a player. But if someone asks for my honest opinion I will give it. I told the director Scott's coaching ideas were very good but didn't always come across that way because he was often grumpy and didn't manipulate the smarter players to his advantage. Scott didn't know how to get the best out of people. It confirmed my theory that the best coaches are those with top man-management skills.

I told the director that Scott just needed to relax and smile a bit more, but they ended up getting rid of him. Even though I'd made my opinions known, I didn't think it was fair that they gave him the push. Scott could have done well if he'd just changed his style. But a few months down the line, I realised that he never really had a chance. Once a club decides they want rid, then you have very little hope of staying on. As I discovered to my own cost.

Anyway, two weeks later I was offered the job of Shaun's assistant on top of playing and captaincy responsibilities. I was made up as I'd been making plans for this moment for ages and had compiled data, going back several years, of training ideas and game tactics etc. I'd also spent two years coaching the Wigan St Pat's amateur open-age team and loved it, even though it was tiring and time consuming. I was also ready to start my level three coaching badge.

But there were still a few problems stopping me from accepting Salford's offer straight away. I felt sorry for Scott for the way they had pushed him out and didn't know if my playing performances would be affected by spending a lot of time on the coaching side as well, a fear proved right by 2010 going on to be my most disappointing individual season. The third factor, and probably the most annoying, was the fact that Salford told me I wouldn't get any more money, even though they effectively expected me to take on a full-time job on top of playing, week in, week out.

I said I needed to think about it but the answer I got back was pretty uncompromising. I was told that if I didn't do it they would bring somebody else in on a two-year deal and, even though nothing was said, we both knew I was unlikely to get another crack at becoming a coach at Salford. I had been thinking that I might retire at the end of 2010 and knew that coaching jobs don't come up that often. So I told Salford that I would take up their offer. And, man, did my life change then.

Coaching responsibilities took over my world completely, but I was so determined to succeed that I threw myself into it, as I do with everything. I felt I should have got some extra cash, particularly when I was being asked to drive all over the place, fetching and carrying things. But I wanted to do well, so I refused to let it be an issue and vowed that I'd make it work. I was so engrossed that I didn't really appreciate that my new workload was bound to take its toll. And thinking about it now, there's no way it couldn't have had an affect on my playing performances; I was driving myself into the ground.

I would arrive at the club between 5.30 and 7.00 in the morning to get ready for the video review sessions and set up everything we needed for training, so that when the lads came in it would all be perfect and ready to go. I probably did far more than was necessary, but that's just the way I am. I'm a perfectionist when it comes to work and it stopped me seeing as much of Sonia and the kids as I should have.

Even if we'd been playing at somewhere like Hull on a Friday night and I hadn't got to bed until 3.00, I'd still be back at the club by 7.00, going through all the DVDs so that our review would be thorough and spot-on straight away. I've sat through too many pointless and badly organised video sessions in the past to know what is needed and what will keep players' attention.

This, for example, was a typical pre-season day. In at the club by 7.00 at the latest. Set everything up for a prompt start to training. A typical training session would include 200 metre sprints in blocks of five, along with skills work. I would be doing my sprints flat out and, instead of resting in between, would race over to the skills station to oversee the lads there, then race back for another sprint. After training, I'd shower and meet up with Shaun for further planning and review sessions. During the season, these also included time-intensive video work.

It was a constant cycle and I forever felt I was playing catch-up, trying to cram as much into my day as possible before heading home at about 8.00pm. I was never getting any rest. Even on allocated days-off I would go into work and do extra; that's just my personality. But it was a grind that would inevitably lead to burn out. Slowly but surely I lost my main focus, which was to play. I was so busy trying to concentrate on the other lads' training and performances that I forgot about myself. Looking back, my chance to coach came too early. It was madness to think I could do that as well as play.

Once the season started, Shaun tried to get me to ease off a little, as a way of protecting me. But I thought that was unfair on Shaun; he didn't have anyone else on the coaching staff at that point, so I tended to dedicate as much time as I had been doing in pre-season.

Joining the coaching staff was a real eye-opener to what was going on at Salford and I was flabbergasted with a lot of things. As players, you sometimes call coaches for the way they do things and at the Willows we would often get told that we couldn't have a video review session because the system had crashed. I used to think that was bollocks and that Shaun - who disliked video work anyway - and Scott couldn't be arsed to organise it properly. But as soon as I went into coaching I realised just how ridiculously bad their resources were, to the point of not having decent broadband.

The computers were constantly crashing and quite often you would lose your work and have to start from scratch. Shaun is far more diplomatic than me, but if I see there's something wrong I have to complain and I was constantly telling Steve Simms that it needed sorting out. But it all fell on deaf ears. Not that it stopped me complaining. We were playing sport at an elite level and needed the resources to back that up.

The other thing that staggered me about the coaching set-up at Salford was the involvement of Steve Simms as director of football. Steve would insist on meetings at 7.00 even if it didn't suit our coaching plans and, as I said, he also signed players without consulting Shaun, a shocking state of affairs for a Super League coach. But Shaun, diplomatic and laid back, would let Simms get away with far too much because he wanted life to run smoothly without arguments. Simms never had the same control when Karl Harrison was in charge and I wish Shaun had been as strong as Rhino. I firmly believe that a coach should have the final say in which players he gets, how he organises the coaching and runs the side. A director of football should concentrate on administration and stay away from team matters.

The more I saw of how the club was run the more disappointed I got. But, because I wanted to become a successful coach, I carried on railing against the lack of resources and continued to try and compensate through sheer hard graft, being the workaholic that I am. I know the club took advantage of that but, to a point, I didn't mind. I was confident it would all be worth it in the long run, when I eventually became a head coach somewhere. I knew I had the ideas and experience, and because I'd been captain from such a young age, knew my man-management skills were very good. I would never have survived as captain at the age of 19 if I didn't know how to get the best out of players who were far older and better than I was at that stage.

I may not have played well in 2010, but being a coach did help massively in coping with the bitter disappointment of knowing that I might never play again when injury struck. I just threw myself into coaching full-time and didn't have time to dwell on the misery of not being able to play.

It was not a happy environment to work in, though, and there was definitely a culture of back-biting. Things weren't helped either when the club appointed Phil Veivers as another assistant coach at the end of 2010. Straight away, we didn't hit it off. I got the impression that because he had played for Huddersfield and St Helens, and had coached at Huddersfield and Wigan, he thought he was far more experienced than me. I felt he came in and tried to dominate me, but I wasn't having that. Even if I'd spent all my career at Salford, I was still confident in my own ideas and abilities. As a result we had a fair few blow-ups and sometimes they would get that bad Shaun would have to intervene - clearly not something Shaun enjoyed.

I actually felt that Shaun was getting bullied in the way the club didn't allow him to do things his own way and with the interference he had to put up with from above. We were being asked to do more and more administrative-style work, when we should have been spending time on coaching, and Shaun was frustrated at the poor resources. I'll give you an example. At my first coaching session, we only had ten cones to put out. My old mate Paul Highton had started up an after-school coaching course, Primary Sport Solutions, and he actually gave us some cones to use! What other Super League club would have to borrow cones? And from a former player who wasn't even allowed a testimonial game at that? But Shaun was so relaxed I thought he could handle everything.

Looking back, I should have realised he was becoming too stressed out and I should have read the signs better when he began to be grateful that me and Veivers were taking on more of his work. At times he was deflated, had no energy and sometimes would forget what he was saying. Then the fans began to turn on him after our poor start to the 2011 season. But when he suddenly left with stress I was completely shocked. Even though I knew he was struggling with some things, I didn't realise he was under as much pressure as he was and I'm really sorry that I couldn't have done more to help because Shaun is such a loveable bloke.

I strongly believe that Shaun was driven out and I vowed there and then that I wouldn't let anybody push me around in that way. It did actually change me from being a bit of a joker to someone far more serious and I put up a barrier, especially when I was dealing with Steve Simms. It was a barrier that proved useless though when Simms decided that I also had to go.

Simms had always backed me as a coach and used to say I could make it to the top if I wanted. But Steve doesn't like people disagreeing with him and that's where things went wrong. I've never been a yes-man for anybody and believe that if you're given a job to do then you should do it as you see fit, not to keep somebody else happy.

Our first clash came after Shaun went off on sick leave and Phil Veivers had gone back to Australia for his mother's funeral. Simms told the players that I was head coach and then, when I did something he didn't like, told me I was assistant and he was head coach. You never knew where you stood with him.

On the afternoon of our game against Wigan in March 2011, Simms phoned to tell me that Daniel Holdsworth had pulled out with a shoulder injury. He had trained all week, hadn't been to see the physio nor mentioned anything to me about a shoulder injury, so I was a bit annoyed. I phoned Daniel and he said that Simms had said it was fine, so me and Steve then ended up having a disagreement over whether Daniel should be allowed straight back in the team the following week. I believe players should know their positions are at risk if they miss a game, but Steve seemed happy for Daniel to be allowed straight back in. I warned him it was setting a bad precedent and for the following four weeks players pulled out on the day of games. But the only one who got a bollocking off Steve was Rob Parker, who wasn't one of his favourites, when he cried off with genuine illness.

Veivers returned from Australia and Simms was trying to get more hands-on in training, but it was a joke and one day he was telling players to do the opposite of what me and Phil wanted. Not long after, all three of us got asked to meet the chairman, John Wilkinson, because he'd heard that not everything was running smoothly. Once again, I explained the problem truthfully and in full detail, including my opinion that Simms was interfering too much and that the players weren't happy with his involvement. Veivers didn't say much at all until we got out of the meeting and he then told me that I was right to tell John what was happening. I thought he should have backed me up in the meeting, but Veivers can obviously play the politics better than I can and I knew there and then that I had just signed the death warrant on my job. Nobody criticises Simms like that and gets away with it.

I went home and told Sonia and she called me a pillock. But no matter how I looked at it, I couldn't have lived with myself if I hadn't told the truth and stood up for what I believed. I realised Simms would be gunning for me so I told Sonia that I was going to be whiter than white from then on so that there could be no possible grounds for them to get rid of me. How foolish I was to believe that.

I was pure as the driven snow over the next week and flogged myself as usual, putting in the long hours - far longer than either Veivers or Simms - yet I hadn't reckoned on Salford pulling a stunt that even I found incredulous.

After an evening spent going through the match video, I went to work the following morning at 5.30 and began to set everything up as usual for the video and training sessions we had planned. The next person in was the conditioner at 7.30 and just before 9.00, when the players started arriving, Simms and Veivers turned up. Simms came up to me and said something that completely gobsmacked me - 'You're drunk, you'd better go home.'

Now I've been drunk enough times to know when I am and I most definitely wasn't. I hadn't had a drink for days so how could I be? I was so angry that I told him to get the breathalyser from the physio's office and I could prove there and then that I wasn't, but Simms refused and told me to go home. The ridiculous thing was that he'd accused me of being drunk and yet he was happy for me to drive home in my car. Where's the duty of care there?

I was fuming and could quite easily have punched him, but I knew I hadn't done anything wrong so I wasn't going to give him the satisfaction of doing something that really was worth a sacking. The players were arriving and I could tell they knew something had kicked off. That was the most demeaning and embarrassing thing in my life - having to walk away knowing that I hadn't done anything wrong.

I got home, phoned Sonia and my union representative and knew - even though I wasn't drunk - that Simms had won. He'd driven me out. It's something I'm still bitter about to this day.

With Salford City Reds chairman John Wilkinson
in happier times

22

*

The Grip of Depression

uddenly a life that had been chaotically busy turned into a life where hours of interminable boredeom stretched out in front of me. And I didn't know how to cope. It's no exaggeration to say that I went through dark times in those first few weeks after I left Salford.

I was more angry and pissed off at first, but then the frustration took over because I felt that the club wasn't listening to what I had to say. I knew I wasn't lying over what had happened, but I'd had my life turned upside down, my career taken from me and I didn't seem to be able to do anything about it.

If ever I've been at fault over anything, I've always been the type of bloke who holds his hands up and takes the punishment. Just as I did when I lost the captaincy. I cocked up then and took it on the chin because I deserved it. But, to my mind, I had done nothing wrong in the saga that saw me pushed out, apart from stick up for myself and stand up for what I believed was right for the team.

The Devil Within

As the days went on, I began to feel more and more hollow and every day woke up with the same empty feeling. I had to get up to take the kids to school and nursery and then I'd come home where there were jobs I could be doing on the house, but I just couldn't motivate myself to do them. I'd make myself a brew and sit and watch endless hours of boring daytime TV. It certainly wasn't the answer and I don't want to watch another Jeremy Kyle programme in my life, but I couldn't persuade myself to do anything else.

As the days went by I got to a point where I didn't even want to get out of bed. I had to, of course, for the kids. But apart from that, I felt I had nothing else to get up for and didn't have any sort of goal to aim at. I'd sit on the settee, wallowing in feelings of never-ending guilt about what had happened and wonder if I'd thrown everything away. The self pity got deeper and deeper. Not even the thought that I'd somehow got to look after my family could shake me out of my dark mood. If anything it made me worse, because it just felt like too much pressure on my shoulders.

I said earlier in the book that I went completely off the rails, going out on benders as I tried to deal with how my life had gone so horribly wrong. It became a vicious circle that led to rows with Sonia, partly because I was spending an awful lot of money trying to find the answer by drinking and partying - and making myself feel far worse, by the way. Looking back, I realise I should have sought professional help, but I wasn't thinking rationally and had always thought I was a strong character who could sort things out myself. Instead, I offloaded a lot of my frustrations on my good mates and nobody was more helpful, and still is even now, than Shaun McRae.

Shaun isn't your typical good listener - he's too busy talking - but he knew what I was going through because he had suffered with depression himself. Unlike a lot of people who didn't know how to deal with me, Shaun knew what to do. He regularly arranged for us to meet up and he'd let me get all my frustrations out and offer advice. Bit by bit, he helped me to see that I could get through it. Even when I did straighten myself out, Shaun still kept in touch and I really appreciated that. He might not realise it, but he was a major part in my revival and recovery.

The thing I can see now is that, actually, my life wasn't in the mess I thought it was; I still had the three most important things in my life in Sonia and the kids. But at the time I came desperately close to losing them because of the way I dealt with the embarrassment, shame and sheer injustice of losing my job. Thank goodness Sonia helped me come to my senses and get me back on the straight and narrow.

My brother Michael offered me work and gradually I started rediscovering my self-worth and got my motivation back. More importantly, I stopped drinking and life slowly started to get rosier. But although I slowly turned my life back around, the bitterness I still feel about the way Salford treated me, a player who had given them everything for 16 years, is unlikely ever to go away.

In the weeks and months following my exit from Salford, I was involved in an almost endless stream of meetings with my union representative and solicitor in an attempt to come to a settlement with the club. Eventually, we came to a financial 'compromise' and a gagging order prevents me going into detail about that. Suffice to say I think Salford got off very lightly considering what they put me through. It certainly wasn't a golden pay-off - more like just what they owed me anyway, given that I was on a year's contract.

Throughout all the meetings and phone calls, there is one man I never heard from; that was as big a disappointment to me. Chairman John Wilkinson never asked for my side of what had happened and never, it seems, felt he needed to talk to one of the club's greatest ever servants, not to mention a player who had worked unpaid as an assistant coach for him for an entire year. I really thought John was a bigger man than that, but I've come to realise that there are a lot of people you cannot take at face value.

When times are bad, you really find out who your friends are and, as well as my close mates, two people who went out of their way to keep in touch and check that I was coping were Shaun and Adrian Morley. I had never played with Moz but he's a top bloke and one of the game's most genuine people. Salford may have paid me a compromise settlement but they also kicked me in the teeth in ways that I found abhorrent for a club that is supposed to be a professional, elite organisation.

Shortly after I left, I was voted by fans as hooker in a Salford Legends team. You cannot believe how honoured I felt to be recognised by the supporters in that way. But my pride was soon smashed to smithereens when I learned that the club wouldn't allow me back to the Willows for the presentation. Every week, at a 2011 home game, one member of the Legends team was honoured on the pitch at half-time and presented with their commemorative shirt. Mine was collected by Kevin Ashcroft but you can imagine how tainted that award was made to feel by the club's actions. I only hope none of the fans thought I had actually snubbed the presentation.

I shouldn't have been surprised really, given that the club had banned me from going back, but it still hurt deeply when they wouldn't bend their petty rule for the Legends presentation. Just like they wouldn't let me witness the last ever game at the Willows in September 2011. I had grown from a boy into a man on that pitch and enjoyed some of the greatest times of my life there. Yet the club were too nasty to allow me to say a last farewell with the players and fans.

Maybe they didn't realise how much that snub would hurt? Or, more likely, they did and that's exactly why they did it.

Everybody knows that Salford doesn't have the biggest fan base. But to the Salford players, they are some of the most passionate and loyal anywhere in the game. There was no better sound than hearing them sing: 'There's only one Malcolm Alker' and I'll always hold them dear to my heart for the way they supported me, and the team, in bad times as well as good. I only wish I could have said a proper goodbye to them, because the send-off they gave me at the end of 2010, when my playing career came to a halt, was truly emotional. I couldn't play because of my neck injury, but the players formed a tunnel on the pitch for me to walk through with Mason and Madison, and the fans were absolutely fantastic. I may have regretted not leaving the club when I had the chance to join other clubs in the past, but one thing I definitely would have missed if I'd gone is the Salford fans.

I almost went to watch the lads when they played Warrington away in June 2011. Some tickets were arranged for me by my old team-mate Karl Fitzpatrick, who now works for the Wolves. But, in the end, I decided not to go. I didn't want to run into Steve Simms. I wasn't certain I would be able to control my temper if our paths crossed.

Despite not going to watch any games, I tune in to Sky Sports every week for their live matches and have to admit that's the only time when I really miss being involved. A lot of people are surprised when I say I don't generally miss the game, even though the sport was my entire life from the age of 16 to 32. But it's hard to explain just what an unhappy environment Salford had become and I certainly don't miss the feeling that I constantly had to watch my own back.

Also, no matter how good the money was and no matter whether I was a so-called well-known player, I never ever let any of it change me and I know that has helped me cope with life after the game far better than many players would. I have always been just Malcolm Alker, the bloke who still mixes with mates he grew up with, never Malcolm Alker the rugby league player. Being in the spotlight never floated my boat, so being out of it doesn't bother me in the slightest.

Do I miss playing? Yes, to a certain extent, and a couple of Championship clubs started showing interest in me once it became known that I'd been given the all-clear to play again after my neck injury was successfully treated. It's something I'm still seriously considering if I can combine it with regular day-time work.

I also believe I've got a lot to offer as a coach, but know how hard it is to get back into the rugby league circle once you are out of it. Just look how long it took Karl Harrison to get back in after Salford sacked him, and yet I've always rated him as one of England's best home-grown talents.

So I might end up playing again, or coaching at some stage. But I know, too, that I will be just as happy if my life doesn't involve rugby. In 2007, I started a two-year college course in bricklaying, as a back-up in case my playing career suddenly ended. I loved it. I attended classes two nights a week and, on my day off at Salford, would go on site, working for nothing for a building company owned by one of the directors, just so I could gain work experience.

As I've mentioned before, I've always planned ahead and I'm so glad that I've now got other skills to fall back on. In 2009, I set up my own company, Malcolm Alker Contruction Ltd, so I know I'll always be able to look after my family. I might be grafting a lot harder these days but nothing beats me without a fight.

As for Salford's future, I really do wish them well and I'm glad they have finally managed to move into a new stadium. Believe it or not, they were talking about building a new stadium way back in 1995 when I signed my first contract. And the prospect of it was still a massive selling point for the club during the talks for my last two contracts - it just shows how long it has dragged on.

But, although I'm sad that I'm unlikely to ever play there, I'm pleased that they've finally achieved their dream and you've got to give credit to Chairman John Wilkinson for that. He deserves big raps for pursuing it for so long and hopefully the players can pay him back with some good results and success on the pitch.

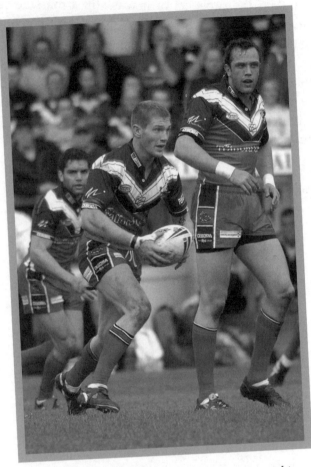

A life after rugby league can be tough to get used to

23

*

Nicked by the Cops - Again!

One of the things I love about working on a building site is the camaraderie between the blokes. It's not that different from the craic that goes on between players in a team. I really enjoy the feeling that everybody's on the same side, working for each other to get results, but having a laugh as well. If you can't have a laugh and a joke at work then life would be pretty miserable and I know more than most how important that is.

As I've said, work helped me to get my sanity back after weeks of hopeless nothingness. Even though I'm a qualified brickie and can turn my hand to plenty of jobs, I quickly realised that finding regular work in the current financial climate was going to be difficult and that's why I'll be forever grateful to my brother Michael for finding me work with him on a major bank refurbishment job he was foreman of in St Helens.

It was a massive help both financially and mentally and gave me some self-esteem back, as well as something to get out of bed for in a morning. It gave me a sense of worth, but boy do these fellas know how to graft. The amount of hours they work is unreal - 19 to 20-hour shifts and that's pure graft, it doesn't include your travel time there and back from home. People might think those sort of hours are not possible, but I soon discovered it's what's expected. If you want to earn a living, that's what you do and I really didn't mind. It was bloody hard, of course, but I was just glad to feel useful again.

Because we were working on a bank, a lot of the work had to be done through the night and that was also a new experience to me. Apart from working late, doing video reviews as a coach, I'd never done anything like that before and it took me a while to adjust. I was getting home at 4.30 or 5.00am and then I'd be up again at 7.00 with the kids. Obviously that couldn't go on and I slowly got used to coping with sleeping during the day. Mind you, I got used to that and then the job got to the stage where we could do more work in the bank during the day as well, so we then started working night and day. But nobody has ever been able to accuse me of not working hard and I'd do whatever was asked of me.

I've always had my eyes open for extra ways to make money and it was agreed that I could take away all the scrap from the bank in my tipper truck each night and flog it. Then I'd buy dinners for the rest of the lads. It seemed a straightforward idea, but it turns out that the police have suspicions about trucks filled with scrap driving at night! The first time I realised this was 4.00 one morning when three police cars flagged me down and surrounded my van. Despite my pleas of innocence, it appears the cops had me down as some sort of tinker on the rob. I guess I did look a bit dodgy.

I'd been arrested once before as a teenager, along with my dad and Melvin, after we were fighting in Wigan one night. We were all put in cells and I decided to play the big man and show I wasn't bothered by urinating on the cell door. But what I didn't realise is that they probably get this quite often. They had put my shoes right outside, in the path of all the piss. I pleaded guilty to a charge of drunk and disorderly and got a £200 fine, whereas Dad and Melvin pleaded not guilty and ended up with £400 fines each, because the fight had been captured on CCTV. At the time, the experience didn't really bother me, but over the years I've grown to realise that it's not worth hassling the police because it will only land you in more trouble.

And so, early that morning last autumn, I said yes sir, no sir, three bags full sir, as the cops insisted on searching through everything in my van for 40 minutes. All I could think of was that I was innocent and knackered and dying to get home to my bed, but I bit my tongue and let them treat me like a suspected criminal until they were satisfied that I hadn't done anything wrong. It happened to me twice more over the next few weeks, but they didn't keep me as long. They radioed my details through and got told that I was legitimate and just trying to earn a living.

A few weeks later, I got another bank job in Birmingham. This time I was in charge, which further boosted my feelings of self-worth and convinced me that I was turning my life around, but in the eyes of the coppers I was the same old suspect villain. Once again I was out in the van, loaded up with scrap and again I got pulled over.

I can also remember my battered old van causing a stir when I turned up at Old Trafford for the traditional pre-season press conference. All the captains had to attend and it was in the days when Andy Farrell was skipper of Wigan. Anyway, I parked up next to this very flash expensive car and out stepped Faz. He did a double take when he realised it was me in the van and even had the nerve to ask if I was driving it for a bet or a giggle. I just laughed at him and told him it was mine - I've never been too proud to let people see me in it. It's partly who I am and there's no need to be ashamed of showing that you're a grafter.

It's quite ironic that the cops suspected me of dodgy dealing because one of my nicknames at Salford was Pikey. It all started when I was in the physio's room one day and I spotted that someone had put a pair of old trainers in a bin. I got them out, announced that there was another six months wear in them and started to wear them. Being a frugal sort, I never miss a trick like that and always claimed boots and trainers that the other players were throwing out.

The other habit that got me a lot of abuse from my team-mates was the way I'd ask any Australian players who were returning home to bring me in any clothes they no longer wanted. I got loads of great clobber that way and it saved me a good few bob. I had no shame, no matter how much stick I got. Mind you, I could still embarrass myself at times with my eye for a bargain, like the time Ian Sibbit and Paul Highton caught me hook, line and sinker with the old glued coin trick. I had been chatting to Shaun McRae outside about a few things ahead of a team meeting. Then, when we got into the changing room and I sat by my peg, I spotted a 50p piece on the floor near my feet. While Shaun took everyone through his game plan and team line-up, I tried to lean over and pick up the money without anyone spotting me. Waste not, want not is my motto. The 50p, though, wouldn't budge. So as not to be beaten I nudged it with my boot - again hoping that no one would see and claim it as theirs. But still it wouldn't move. Not long after that the other players couldn't hold their amusement in any longer and burst out laughing. Shaun was pretty stunned because he wasn't in on the joke and I had to tell him that I'd been rumbled. Not beaten though! After the meeting I went to get a chisel and got the 50p after all.

24

*

Give Us All a Chance

In the autumn of 2011, I was short-listed for the vacant coaching job at Leigh, following Ian Millward's decision to try his luck back in Super League with Castleford. I really thought I was in with a shout.

But the money on offer was poor, certainly not enough to live on, so I told them I would also need time to run my building company. I knew I could successfully juggle the two roles and thought it was still up for negotiation, but the next thing I heard was that they'd offered the job to an overseas guy with little or no coaching experience.

I was disappointed naturally, but not heartbroken. My building business was beginning to take off, even though I did seem to be working all the hours that God sends - I did 22 hours in one stretch, caught about four hours' kip and then started all over again. But the overriding emotion when I heard the news was frustration, because there was no way on earth that Leigh would have offered this other bloke the money they had dangled in front of me. He wasn't going to move his family from the other side of the world to accept the job on the terms that I'd been offered. Also, on top of his salary, the club would presumably have also had to pay for his and his family's flights, a car for him and a house to live in. The maths just didn't add up and it was me who seemed to have been offered the rough deal. In my opinion, that's because I'm English and when it comes to English coaches there seems to be this belief that they'll never be as good as Aussie coaches.

It really makes my blood boil because some relatively unknown and untested Aussies keep getting chances over here and yet our homegrown talent often doesn't get a look in. We've got some good coaches in this country but they're not being allowed to show how good they might be. And nobody will ever convince me that it's better to appoint an Aussie who doesn't know the game over here, or most of the players, and doesn't have a network of people he can turn to for advice, information or to pick their brains.

I really believe there should be some legislation in place stating that all lower league clubs have to have British coaches because that is the only way that we are going to develop our own coaches. If the lower league clubs, as well as most of the Super League clubs, keep turning to Australia to find their coaches then our own people are going to be lost forever and that's not right.

I've seen more than my fair share of Aussies in my time who hate the weather conditions over here and struggle to cope. But it's not just the weather that they'll find different. Some Aussies don't appreciate that a lot of players live some distance away and the travelling that can be involved. For instance, if a coach tries to follow the Aussie system of getting players in early for a morning session, followed by a long break and then an afternoon session, he automatically subjects them to long journeys at peak hours at both ends of the day. That can add up to four hours a day in the car which can lead to hamstring and back problems. Also most Super League clubs don't have the recovery facilities that exist in the NRL. At Salford, our rest-room was little more than a classroom with hard chairs - no comfy chairs, TV or darts to stimulate the players. Long recovery sessions could end up with players just drinking coffee and eating biscuits to wile away the time and that is counter-productive. Some Aussie coaches find these set-ups hard to deal with.

The above problems relate to full-time players, and for part-time players there are even more things to handle. If a club brings over an Aussie coach, he will invariably be full-time and yet he's dealing with players who are playing more as a hobby, fitting it in around the work that earns them their living. Some Championship players are only on a few thousand quid, so their main job naturally has to come first. Yet some coaches find it difficult dealing with players who have worked all day, often doing hard manual labour, and then come into training knackered. Coaches will want them to train four or five times a week, as well as play, but that can be tough with a full-time job and family to look after.

Although my coaching career at Salford was relatively brief, and mostly as the number two, I am convinced that I have got all the attributes to be a head coach and to make a club a success. And I'm not just talking short term. I have got a lot of ideas about how clubs, as well as teams, should be run and I'll keep a lot of them secret because at some point I'm hoping I'll still get chance to put them into practice. But one of the things I was very keen to introduce at Leigh was a system of monthly coaching sessions with all the amateur coaches in the area. I would have gone through coaching techniques, video analysis and everything to broaden their horizons and hopefully help Leigh in the long run. These amateur coaches are nurturing some of the stars of the future and I felt that it would help enormously if we could sign up young players who had already been introduced to mine and Leigh's way of thinking and playing. A long-term plan but I truly believe that a club of Leigh's size and stature should be looking at ideas like this.

As far as coaching ideas go, I would happily back mine against anybody's because I've already got the proof to put my money where my mouth is. Just after Shaun went off ill, Salford played Wigan and I came up with a gameplan where we were going to target full-back Sam Tomkins with high kicks, not because he is a bad catcher of the ball, but because it would allow our players time to close him down before he had chance to run with it and launch one of his dangerous counter-attacks. Steve Simms ripped the idea to shreds and overruled me, telling the team to kick to the corners instead - a textbook tactic basically. It's fair enough a lot of the time, but when you've got a player like Tomkins who is so good at reading plays and getting into the right positions then I believed we had to come up with something different. I was convinced my idea would have worked so how I chuckled to myself in November when I watched the Four Nations Final. Guess what, Australia came up with the exact same plan. It worked a treat and everybody was raving about how clever the Aussies were to nullify the threat from Tomkins. Seems I did know what I was talking about after all. Maybe if I'd been an Aussie, no questions would have been asked.

The week before that Wigan game, when Shaun was still at the club, I was in charge of the attacking gameplan for our match against Wakefield. I devised an idea that I admit was a bit out of the box, but one I was convinced would work. All teams target a certain side, usually a particular unit rather than an individual player, in the hope of attracting players in so that space opens up around them. Also fatigue will eventually affect that unit and weaknesses will start to show. My idea was to keep swapping our left and right side players over, so that fresh players kept working over that particular unit of the opposition, in the hope of making them fatigued far more quickly. Shaun wasn't too happy and didn't want to do it, but I eventually persuaded him to let me have a go, saying that we had already lost our opening two matches so surely it was worth us trying something else. I then told the players of the gameplan and some of the senior ones were taken aback; you could tell they thought I'd lost the plot. I urged them not to be suspicious just because it was new, so we ran with it and I'm pleased to say it worked like a dream. We kept swapping around our players, but working the same side, and in the last 20 minutes we ran away with the game and won 32-6, partly because Wakefield were so tired. After the game, Luke Patten, who had been one of the senior players to voice his doubts, came up and told me that he was surprised how effective it had been. Luke has played at a high level and so I was really glad that he'd actually admitted he thought it a good idea. He didn't have to, but the fact that he took the effort to do that was a real pat on the back for me.

I always like to try and come up with different game-plans and ideas and I'm sure all the other up-and-coming coaches in this country have their own ideas as well. But, while ever clubs seem to have this love affair with Aussie coaches, we run the risk of stifling and eventually killing off a lot of our talent. At the moment we've got a few English coaches who are trying valiantly to break through, but rugby league people are proud and eventually a lot of them will say 'sod it, why bother?' Over the next five or six years we'll certainly start to see a lack of young British coaches coming through. And who can blame them when they see the quality of some of the Aussie coaches who are getting jobs? At least Leigh eventually settled on giving local

201

stalwart Paul Rowley the role, after he had initially been in caretaker charge.

Some of those blokes have been dire, but it's not just coaches, it's Aussie players as well. We've had some terrible ones at Salford. I remember a lad called Mick Burn who was shocking. He had feet for hands and even Salford realised he was too bad to play him too often. And yet this was a lad who the club had forked out on flights and digs for, as well as his salary. We could have had two or three British lads for what they had paid out for him.

While clubs often fall over themselves to take a gamble on anybody with an Australian passport, they don't seem quite as keen to put their faith in young English kids. Take 20-year-old prop Jack Spencer, for example. Here was a lad who was Salford through and through, having supported them all his life, and he just needed nurturing and a decent coach to bring the best out of him. But at the end of last season Matt Parish fired him off, saying he didn't think he was good enough. A few weeks later Tim Sheens and Wests Tigers came in for Jack - and you can't tell me that Sheens doesn't know a thing or two about players.

25

*

Good and Evil

It was weird when we were thinking of names for the book and the suggestion of *The Devil Within* was made. I couldn't believe the coincidence because I'd already made an appointment with my tattooist to have those very words tattooed at the top of my left arm, underneath the picture of a devil appearing to fight its way out of my skin.

Maybe it was destiny. The title works on so many levels, partly because of my long association with Salford, the original Red Devils, and also because I've struggled at various stages in my life to control the devil that lurks inside me and had trouble stopping it from causing havoc in my life. As you know, I've not always managed to keep the devil contained! Everybody probably has one, but other people seem to know how to tame theirs.

But, to show that it's a battle I want to win, I also asked my tattooist, a wonderful bloke call Saz in Irlam, to do a picture of two angels at the top of my right arm to show that it's a fight between good and evil. Also on that theme of good and bad, I've got a tattoo of an unhappy face on my left hand and one of a happy face on my right hand. Whenever I feel I need inspiration I'll look at my right hand and remind myself that happiness is the way forward - and of what I need to do to achieve that.

I know they're not everyone's cup of tea, but I love my tattoos and have done ever since I got my first one at the age of 14. Yes, I know the legal age is 18, but I'd been told of a tattooist in a back street in Wigan who wouldn't ask any questions and, sure enough, when I turned up looking relatively fresh faced he never batted an eyelid or asked me anything about my age.

My first tattoo was a bulldog's head with big green eyes and a collar, on the top of my right leg. I couldn't afford to have the body tattooed as well, so I just had the head and the poor old bulldog has copped a lot of stick since from team-mates who think it's hilarious that I've only got a dog's head and no body. But I still love it and from that first tattoo there's been no looking back. It's probably going to be a work in progress for years to come.

I didn't tell my parents about that first tattoo. But I knew I wanted more, so I started mentioning them to my mum and, even though she was against the idea at first, I slowly talked her round. When I was 15, she even agreed to come with me when I had an eagle tattooed on my shoulder. She, of course, thought she was being supportive of my first one - an idea only crushed some time later when I accidentally had my shorts pulled down during a game and she saw the bulldog!

Since then the tattoos have spread over most of my arms, and me and all three brothers have got the word 'family' in Korean on our right wrist and 'brothers' on our left. I've also got my kids' and Sonia's names; the crucifiction with Jesus to symbolise the sacrifices I've made for my family; LOVE on my knuckles following my escape from drug addiction, plus 'loyalty' on my chest, although Salford have tainted that word a bit for me.

I've only regretted one - a bulldog on my arm that ended up looking more like a bat - and I'm currently going through the lengthy process of having that lazered off. It takes about half an hour of lazering and you then have to let that scab over before you go back six weeks later for more. That goes on numerous times before it's gone. I'll be glad when it's off so I can plan something new and better.

Another naff one I had was 'Mad Monday 07' on my backside, but at least not many people see that one. I was out with Karl Fitzpatrick, Stuart Littler and Gareth Haggerty on Mad Monday when Fitzy suggested we all get one. I texted Sonia to tell her and she texted back 'no way', so I turned my mobile off and had it anyway.

Who'll play number nine in my Willows Dream Team?
Who do you think?

26

*

My Salford Dream Team

My time at Salford ended in disappointment, but that doesn't mean the club won't always hold a special place in my heart. Here is my choice of the 13 best players I lined up alongside at the Willows.

FULL BACK - KARL FITZPATRICK
Fitzy was a real elusive runner, very good under the high ball, a great support player and top tackler. His height probably let him down a bit as a full-back, but he would never pull out of anything. He's a really tough guy and was 100 per cent committed to anything he did.

WINGERS - MICHAEL HANCOCK, MARTIN OFFIAH
Aussie international Michael Hancock was very, very strong and fast. He had great footwork and a wealth of experience when he joined Salford, but nearly every day after training he would go out on his own and do more training.

Martin Offiah is also in my Super League dream team

and an absolute legend. He scored so many tries for us, many of them absolute crackers.

CENTRES - STUART LITTLER and AARON MOULE

I couldn't resist putting Stu into my nutcase team, but there's no doubt that he belongs in a Salford dream team too. He was a fantastic tackler and a good runner who could be guaranteed to hit very good lines, also very durable. Stu still holds the Salford record for most consecutive appearances: 163. Stu had to be dying before he'd miss a game.

Aaron Moule had a terrific step on him and was very good at creating space for his winger. His only downfall was that he was a little injury-prone. Other than that, he was a top player. Aaron was also a bit of a deep thinker and is now travelling Europe working as a personal trainer.

STAND OFF - DANIEL HOLDSWORTH

An exceptional player with bucketloads of talent. Can tend to do his own thing on the field, but if he was playing with Gavin Clinch, who could organise better, then those two would make a super half-back pairing. Unusually tall for a stand-off, but that helps to make his defence even better.

SCRUM HALF - GAVIN CLINCH

Another player who is also in my Super League dream team. Gavin was sheer class and deserved more recognition than he probably got.

PROPS - PAUL HIGHTON and CRAIG STAPLETON

I've come across a lot of good props, but with Highto you always knew exactly what you were going to get - solid foundations. He would always be in the right position defensively. As a coach, you knew so well what Highto was going to provide that it helped the rest of your selection.

Craig Stapleton is another top class prop who is also deservedly in my Super League dream team.

HOOKER - Me of course!

SECOND ROW - JASON NICHOL and IAN SIBBITT

Jason Nichol started as a centre when he came over from Australia, but switched to the back row and did really well. Good step, great fend and generally a superb all-round player. Really nice bloke as well.

Ian Sibbitt is a very good runner of the ball and hits a great line. I would jump out at hooker and instinctively know that Sibs would be there supporting. It takes a lot to run off the ball like he did.

LOOSE FORWARD - DARREN BROWN

Great hands and a terrific finisher as well as a top organiser, tackler and kicker. Darren's defence could be hit and miss but that was outweighed by the attacking opportunities he created. I reckon he was a few years ahead of his time. If he was playing nowadays he'd have been sensational.

COACH - KARL HARRISON

Rhino brought a load of ideas with him when he took over at Salford and opened our eyes as to how professional the players - and the club - had to be. He took us to our highest finishing spot of fifth. It's just a pity that we couldn't step up from that level.

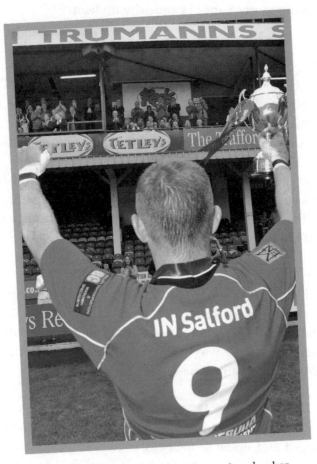

It takes a certain personality type to be a hooker

27

*

Happy Hookers

Hookers are the equivalent to many goalkeepers in football teams - slightly crazy and definitely unstable. And believe me, I'm talking from first hand experience. I don't know what it is about the position but it is definitely one that attracts blokes who, putting it politely, like to live life to the full! But no matter how mad we might be, I cannot let this book go without paying tribute to some sensational hookers who have graced our game.

Still entertaining us is James Roby, undoubtedly one of the best hookers in the world and one who I'd have in my team ahead of great Australian hooker Cameron Smith any day. Smith has won just about everything and he probably deserves it, but remember who he's got around him in that pack. Who couldn't play well with those sort of players? Smith's best attribute is probably his kicking game and he's certainly a better kicker than Roby, who has got a strong long kick on him but isn't as accurate. But apart from that, I believe Roby is better in every other facet of the game.

The Devil Within

Roby isn't that big but he has the most amazing strength and an unbelievable engine on him. He just keeps kicking, tackling, running all match long and that's why he probably goes unnoticed to a degree; everybody now expects him to have those high standards every single game. Other players might get the accolades but Roby makes St Helens tick. Next time you watch Saints, notice Roby coming off the pitch at the end. I'll bet he's the dirtiest player out there and that's because of the incredible workload he gets through.

Roby, of course, took over from Keiron Cunningham and how lucky Saints are to have had two of the modern day great hookers. The fact that they built a statue of Keiron in St Helens while he was still playing shows just what a legend he is. He was a fantastic runner and so quick, a good passer of the ball, although he was a bit dodgy with his left to right pass, and a real top powerhouse. One of the greatest.

Looking a little further back, James Lowes stands out as another fantastic number nine. Jimmy has always been a real in-depth thinker about the game - usually outside the box - and I learnt a lot from him in that respect. When he was coaching us at Salford he would always keep the players stimulated because he's very smart and knows what players will respond to. As a player he was a great passer of the ball, had a terrific kicking game and good vision, as well as being very tough. People will say he played behind an awesome pack at Bradford and that's true. There's no doubt that they helped his game, but Jimmy helped theirs too.

Going even further back and I watched Wigan's Martin Dermott in awe, as a kid. If anything, he was slightly ahead of his time. He was one of the greatest passers of the ball but it was his feet that had me entranced. When he went down to pass the ball he would change his footwork and, even as a kid, I could see how that subtle shift helped his passing accuracy and service. That's one of the most overlooked aspects of the game, but I used to love watching him do it and vowing one day that I would try to be just as good.

Lee Jackson is another who gets my vote for his explosive style of play, his vision and as a great runner of the ball. But Lee is another example of how hookers can thrive when they play in teams that are big and fast. Lee always seemed to have good armoury around him, wherever he played, and that is always a hooker's dream.

One of the more famous hookers, of course, is Mick Stephenson, who was part of the 1972 World Cup winning side, sadly the last time this country has managed to win a major series or tournament. Stevo certainly deserves credit for that, but his fame also partly comes from the fact that he repeatedly harps on about hookers on Sky TV. I have to admit, I can't bear listening to him and mute the volume when he's on. He infuriates me because he's still saying the same things he was ten years ago and yet the game has moved on so much.

For anybody like me, who loves the technical side of the game, he's a joke and makes me cringe. I know Sky like him to be controversial, and he might seem to make sense to a lot of viewers, but he drives a lot of players and coaches mad.

I also remember him awarding me the man of the match award after one game and then, three weeks later, Salford were on Sky again. This time he absolutely panned me, saying I was gone and past it as a player. I'm sure he had forgotten that he had been raving about me three weeks earlier, but that's Stevo for you.

I was known for my tackling -
but there was more to my game than that

28

*

Player Welfare

Writing this, highlighting all the ups and downs, has forced me to look at my career with a scrutiny that I never did when I was a player. At the time, you become so engrossed in trying to keep your place in the team, and at times in just trying to survive the pain and rigours of training, that you don't look at the bigger picture. That's one reason players get sucked into problems with prescription pain-killers, not to mention the evils of social drugs and booze. Of course, not everybody succumbs to these things, and good luck to them. But there are certainly a lot who do and I truly believe that more needs to be done to help them. In November 2011, the RFL announced a new player welfare programme to be introduced at all Super League clubs over the following two years; long overdue.

It's players like me, who have gone through just about every experience - good and bad - who should be encouraged to help current players with their problems. Before the RFL initiative, which is well intentioned but will take time to take effect, player welfare was something that I believe came too far down the list of priorities within the sport.

When I finished at Salford I got a voice message on my mobile from a welfare officer at the RFL asking me to ring her if I had any problems I wanted to discuss. Now, with the best will in the world, that was never going to happen. Even though I knew I was in a bit of trouble with depression and going off the rails, there was no way I was going to ring some woman I didn't know and confess that I had lost my way... that I was in danger of throwing away my home life because I couldn't handle what had happened to me.

I was fairly certain she would never have experienced first hand the highs of playing, and the lows of losing your career, never mind the personal battle I was having at the time with my drug and booze dependency. But if I had thought that the person who had made that call was an ex-player, who had gone through similar experiences and knew where I was coming from, then maybe I would have opened my heart and asked for help. Yet there was nothing in place like that because the RFL doesn't seem overly keen on using its best resources - the players - once they have finished playing.

The game loves players when they are helping to make it a success but there seems to be little in place for players when their careers come to an end, either through retirement or injury. From my experience, there has been very little in the way of a support mechanism to make sure these players don't go off the rails, or suffer depression, or fall on hard times because they no longer know how to make a living. And it does happen, far more than people realise. Hopefully, the new welfare programme, which will help players plan their financial futures as well as future career and job prospects, will ease some of the problems that have existed.

Of course, in an ideal world, players would plan for

when rugby league is over and make provisions for a new career or job. But, as we all know, life isn't always like that and a lot of lads reach the end with nothing really in place. Many rugby players neglect their schooling to some degree because they start playing the game to a high level at an early age and set their hearts on making it as a professional sportsman. That may seem fine when you are running around in the spotlight and earning decent money, but it can be disastrous when you've hung up the boots and need to find some other way to pay the mortgage.

I was lucky enough to have the nous to plan and get a secondary career, with my bricklaying and construction business, but I've thought long and hard about this and believe it's a problem that should, and can, be solved. The game should be looking at giving kids an education, or a trade, so that they have something to fall back on if they get injured and have to retire, or even if their club decides they are no longer good enough to earn a contract. For the older players, that need is even more important. I don't think it's unfair to expect the game gradually to reinstate them back into society, by giving them a helping hand with training, education or even financial help if they fall on hard times.

At the moment, it's almost like players are numbers on a factory floor and, when your time is up, you are discarded and forgotten about. That's not fair on people who have given a lot to rugby league and it's also a shameful waste of talent and experience. I'm sure we could stamp out at least some of the drink and drugs problems if players knew there were a number of ex-pros they could turn to for advice and help. I would be delighted to do that sort of job, and I would hope I could prevent players making a lot of the mistakes I did. I would certainly have listened to such advice if I knew it came from someone who had faced similar problems as me at various points in my career. But, if such a system is introduced, there needs to be a level of secrecy about it. Players need to know that if they confess to having a drink or drug dependency, it won't result in punishment or a ban from the game. Education and help is what is needed.

Depression is another big area that needs tackling and I was really heartened to see that one round of fixtures, at the end of 2011, was designated as the State of Mind weekend. Terry Newton's tragic death lit a spark and it's just a real shame that it needed something as heartbreaking as that to make people aware of the issue. But at least something is now being done and that can only be good. From my own experience, I know all too well how depression can take over your life and almost wreck it - and your family life - if you are not careful.

I have been through the whole gamut of problems - drugs (legal and illegal), drink and depression. So who better to help players facing similar problems? But if not me, then the RFL certainly needs to think about bringing in other ex-players. There are too many of us going to waste.

29

*

Out for the Count

Some readers might be wondering why I haven't written much so far about my reputation as one of Super League's best ever tacklers.

I topped the tackle count in 2001, 2002, 2005 and 2009, winning the Super League Hitman of the Season award in those years, and I was the first player to pass 1,000 tackles in a season. I admit that I'm proud of those achievements. But you may also be surprised to learn that I think my prowess ended up as a bit of a stigma, rather than something to boast too much about.

I'm not saying that tackling isn't a vital part of the game but I think my reputation may also have actually held my international ambitions back a little. It's great to be known as a fearless and effective tackler and defender and in Australia that is key - everything else springs from a solid defence. But over here we play a different game and the attacking side of a player's armoury is deemed more important. In Australia, they pride themselves on defence, over here it's seen as a lesser option compared to other parts of the game.

So I never went into games thinking I wanted to make a certain number of tackles, instead I always went in with the ambition of getting to run the ball at least once in every set of six. It sometimes didn't work, but that was always my primary aim. The tackling just happened because a lot of opponents dominated Salford, so I was naturally having to do a lot of tackles, and also teams tend to run at one of the pivotal players, the hooker or either of the half-backs, and so that also played a part in me racking up the tackles.

Also, before Shaun McRae arrived at the club, I would play the full 80 minutes, so that helped my tackle count as well. Shaun introduced the idea of rotating two hookers and I didn't like that because it didn't suit my game. For 12 years I'd been used to playing 80 minutes and I always felt my energy levels grew as the game went on. Having spells on the bench totally disrupted me and I found that system very hard to adjust.

Luke Adamson, one of Salford's brightest young stars, is another who racks up huge tackle counts every game, but when I was at the club I tried really hard to try and stop him from putting too much importance on it. It's not the be all and end all. I tried to help him develop other aspects of play, telling him that he didn't want to end up with the same reputation I'd had. All Luke's extras in training were on his attack, his landing positions, spinning in the tackle and two-handed carries in the hope that he'd get the right combination of attributes to earn him the international success that I missed out on.

So yes, it may surprise people that arguably the aspect I'm best known for isn't a major thing in my life. But there again, I don't think I do the expected in a lot of things. I've met many a former player who likes to live on past glories, but that's not for me. When I started a new building job in November 2011, I was working with a guy who kept telling me how he used to play amateur rugby a fair bit. He hadn't a clue who I was, but he obviously liked to mention his playing days and I just kept quiet, listening to his chatter. About ten days later one of the other lads finally told him who I was and, once it was pointed out, he actually knew me because he was from Sale and had watched Salford over the years. But to be honest, I couldn't care less whether people know or not. I certainly don't worry about wanting my place in rugby league history.

All I hope is that people have been entertained by my stories and know that I have been brutally honest for a reason. One, there's no point in writing an autobiography if you aren't honest. And two, I sincerely hope my revelations about drugs and other problems in rugby league will result in improvements for players.

Now that's a legacy I would be proud of.

Scratching Shed Publishing Ltd - Bringing history to life

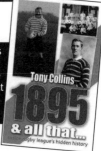

Scratching Shed Publishing Ltd

Scratching Shed Publishing Ltd is an independent publishing company founded in May 2008. We aim to produce high-quality books covering a wide range of subjects - including sport, travel and popular culture - of worldwide interest yet with the distinctive flavour of the North of England.

Coming soon:
In the summer of 2012
John Kear - The Autobiography